# GRIEF
### AND
# GRIEVING

## Understanding Grief and the Grieving Process

### First Edition

Horizon Publishing
Horizon Consulting and Productions
www.horizpro.com

Grief and Grieving
Understanding Grief and the Grieving Process

ISBN 10: 0985328401    ISBN 13: 978-0-9853284-0-5

Front Cover Artwork: © rolffimages – Fotolia.com
Back Cover Design: © Lulu Templates. Lulu.com
Photo and Graphics: © Daniel Wheeler
Author: Daniel Wheeler
Contributors: Reverend Doctor Mara Leigh "Coach" Taylor, Dr. Melvin M. Moore Ph.D.
Publisher: Horizon Publications; a subsidiary of Horizon Consulting and Productions.
Published in the United States of America
First Printing: Lulu.com
Print is last number listed:
10  9  8  7  6  5  4  3  2  1

For questions, email: info@horizpro.com
Or write to: Daniel Wheeler/Horizon Consulting
P.O. Box 283, Lomita, CA 90717, USA

Disclaimer:

Daniel Wheeler makes no claims, promises, or guarantees about the accuracy, completeness or adequacy of the information contained herein. This book and the information contained herein are for educational and inspirational purposes only and not to be used for self-treatment. The information is not intended or implied to be a substitute for professional medical advice or a replacement for any treatment. Daniel Wheeler assumes no responsibility for any circumstances arising out of the use, misuse, interpretation, or application of any information herein. Always seek the advice of a physician or qualified health provider for all medical or psychological problems, treatments, or with questions regarding any medical or psychological condition.

# GRIEF
### And
# GRIEVING

# Understanding Grief and the Grieving Process

## Daniel Wheeler R.H., CHt., C.S.C.

Horizon Publishing
Horizon Consulting and Productions
www.horizpro.com

I dedicate this book in loving memory to my mother…

# Pasqualina

There is no other more gentle or precious than thee, and memories don't pass away so easily.

# Table of Contents

# Acknowledgements

During the past several years of researching and writing this book on grief and the grieving process, and in my endeavors to gather knowledge on the subject of self-improvement over the many years that I have been a hypnotherapist, life coach, and spiritual counselor, I have explored many diverse ideas and areas of self-awareness. I have studied and read many books on the subject, attended classes and workshops, and researched information from many sources. I have exchanged ideas and information with colleagues and friends, and with fellow students and clients. It would be impossible to name them all here, but I would like to acknowledge them all for their contributions and support through the years, and for expressing to me the need to develop a book and workshop that clearly defines the grief and grieving process in easy to understand layperson terms.

I would like to thank Coach Mara Leigh Taylor for suggesting that I, as a Community Volunteer, teach a self-awareness class to her students at the Getting Out by Going In

(GOGI) Campus, from which a need for a definitive class on the grief and grieving process became so apparent. My gratitude and appreciation to her for the many wonderful lessons, insights, and opportunities she has so graciously extended to me. I would also like to extend my appreciation to Dr. Melvin M. Moore for his contributions, friendship, guidance, and wisdom.

I have researched, to the best of my ability, ownership and copyright for the material obtained on-line through research, dictionary, encyclopedia, and public domain sites, and when at all possible and available, given credit to the authors or creators of the information I have used in this book. If I have left anyone out, it was not intentional, and I thank you all for your wisdom and knowledge.

I thank my wonderful sister for always being there for me when I needed an encouraging word or two. Most of all I thank my beautiful wife for her patience, understanding, and support. I thank her for helping me cope while on my own journey through the grief and grieving process.

# Preface

Grief and grieving is a personal journey that we all will face, in our own ways, one time or another, in our lives. Any time we experience a loss, whether it is the death of a loved one, the loss of a job or home, a divorce or separation, loss in status or lifestyle, our freedom, or health, some degree of grief will naturally occur. At the time of the loss, we may or may not be aware of how it can and does affect our emotions or well being, and many times we are far along in the grief and grieving process before we take appropriate steps to understand and accept the process and our reactions to our loss.

This book is designed to give the reader a general understanding of what grief is and how the grieving process works. By recognizing how grief is manifested and where it comes from, as well as the process of grieving, one can use the faculties of one's mind to navigate through the process of grief and grieving with a better understanding and with better tools for coping. Grieving is a personal experience. In this book, I have purposely left out individual's testimonials and personal stories of grief and loss, which are often times included in books about the subject of grief and grieving. I think that we create our own individual stories about our journey and our experiences, as thought provoking and revealing as they are. You will undoubtedly have a few stories of your own to tell at some point along your journey.

Depending on the individual, (who you are) and the nature of your loss, the grief and grieving process can manifest itself in many different forms and degrees of severity; from simple feelings of loss, loneliness, and acceptance, to complex and deep rooted pain, anguish, depression, and addiction. The chapters in this book cover the many facets of grief and grieving and offer personal exercises and ideas for coping with and embracing your personal grief or grieving. These exercises and coping ideas can also be used in a group setting, when loss and change affects groups of individuals in the same way due to similar circumstances, or when a group of individuals experiences similar situations and trauma.

I hope that through the use of this book on grief and grieving, you will find the gateway to your inner peace and freedom and find relief from your pain and sadness or yearning, fear, worry, anxiety or anger, helplessness and hopelessness, or depression, so that you can peacefully and easily find personal acceptance, and come to terms with your loss.

I encourage you to discuss your feelings of grief and grieving with someone you trust, such as a member of the clergy, rabbi, chaplain, counselor, or a health professional. It is perfectly acceptable and important to get the support that you need.

The author Daniel Wheeler does not attempt to treat or diagnose disease or mental disorders of any kind. The information throughout the chapters in this book is not intended or implied to be a substitute for professional medical advice or a replacement for any treatment. Always seek the advice of a physician or qualified health provider for all medical or psychological problems, treatments, or with questions regarding a medical or psychological condition, especially when severe or complicated grief symptoms manifest themselves. As stated previously, this book is designed to give the reader a general understanding of what grief is and how the grieving process works. It is for educational and inspirational purposes only and not to be used for self-treatment. It is not a substitute for professional medical services or treatments.

Please take the information, personal exercises, and ideas for coping, provided in this book, to use as you see fit. Some of the information may be helpful, some of the information you may already have working knowledge of, and some of the information hopefully will be transformational, providing you the reader, with a better understanding of the journey through the process of grief and grieving.

# A Breeze on Butterfly Wings

Whence comes the wind that blows gently
through the trees…and where does it go?

Yet in its gentle passing do we not feel it's soft
velvet touch upon our cheeks?

Like the flutter of butterfly wings….first
sensed and now lost.

For all its reality, we cannot reach out and
touch or grasp the wind.
It is there…yet it is not.

How real too is our sense of sight?
When we see in our dreams our loved ones
who have passed?

Again we see them….and talk to them…and
walk…and love again.

Yet are they there?  Will they come when we
call?   Yes…and yes again…it is true.

~ Daniel Wheeler

# ❧ CHAPTER ONE ❧
## Grief and Grieving

"There are as many nights as days, and the one is just as long as the other in the year's course. Even a happy life cannot be without a measure of darkness and the word 'happy' would lose its meaning if it were not balanced by sadness."   ~ Carl Gustav Jung

## Grief and Grieving

Grief is your emotional reaction to a significant loss. The words sorrow and heartache are often used to describe feelings of grief. Whether you lose a beloved person, animal, place, object, or a valued way of life (such as your job, your freedom, your marriage, your social standing, or good health), some level of grief will naturally follow.

Grieving is the process of emotional and life adjustment that you go through after a loss. Grieving after a loved one's death is also known as bereavement. Grieving is a personal experience. Depending on whom you are and the nature of your loss, your process of grieving will be different from another person's experience. There is no "normal" or "expected" period of time for grieving. Some people adjust to a new life within several weeks or months. Others take a year or more, particularly when their daily life has been radically changed or their loss was traumatic and unexpected. Some experience grief for a lifetime, especially without the proper understanding of the feelings, emotions, and process that they are going through. A radical change in lifestyle can bring on grief and grieving. When you're whole world and perspective changes, there normally follows a period of loss, sorrow, and sadness.

A wide range of feelings and symptoms are common during grieving. While feeling shock, numbness, sadness, anger, guilt, anxiety, or fear, you may also find moments of relief, peace, or happiness. While grieving is not simply sadness, or "the blues", you may become depressed or overly anxious during the grieving process.

The stress of grief and grieving can also have a physical affect on your body. Sleeplessness is common, as is a weakened immune system over time. If you have a chronic illness, grieving can at times make your condition worse. We often think of grief as strictly an emotional process, but grief often involves physical problems, including fatigue, nausea, as previously stated, lowered immunity, weight loss or weight gain, aches and pains, and insomnia (sleeplessness).

Many independent and institution funded studies have been conducted on the affects of grief on the autoimmune, endocrine, autonomic nervous, and cardiovascular systems, with varying results. I recommend discussing your concerns with a medical doctor before coming to any conclusions, or relating any physical or medical conditions to symptoms of grief or grieving.

Grief and loss can affect your overall health. It can lead to depression and even, at times, excessive alcohol or drug use. Grief that lasts for several months and is severe enough to interfere with daily life, may be a sign of a more serious illness, such as major depression. Psychological counseling and physician prescribed medication can be helpful and very effective when battling severe depression.

Although it may be possible to postpone grieving, it is not possible to avoid grieving altogether. If life circumstances make it difficult for you to stop, feel, and live through the grieving process, you can expect grief to eventually erupt sometime in the future. In the meantime, unresolved grief can affect your quality of life and relationships with others.

While grieving is difficult and painful, it does not have to immobilize us. We can learn to be patient with ourselves and with others during periods of grief, by understanding what we are going through.

If we understand the processes that are taking place in our minds, and the reasons for our feelings of grief and loss, we can start the healing process. What should you expect while you are coping with grief? How will you react? Do you feel tense? Do you feel anxious? Remember that crying is a healthy release of tension and anxiety. Pretending to be strong and showing no emotions is not only difficult, but it represses your feelings, often hiding them away, only to have them rush forward like a volcano erupting at a later time, and in a way, that you do not expect. You may also experience loss of appetite, sleeplessness, lack of concentration, and fatigue. If you turn to alcohol and drugs as a way to cope with your grief, they will only mask and delay the grief process, so consider avoiding them during this time. It is also wise not to make major decisions or take on new responsibilities until your grief has subsided.

Many people experience a myriad of reactions during the process of grieving. If your pain and sorrow is especially intense, you may even lose interest in life itself. In order to safeguard yourself against a long period of depression as a result of grief, it is very important to find purpose and activities outside of yourself and your present circumstances. In time, your sense of purpose will return as the pain and sorrow becomes less intense.

You may also experience guilt and find yourself asking, "How could I allow this to happen"? Learning to forgive yourself and others is an important factor in overcoming this thought cycle. Knowing that you are doing the best that you can, and that some things are out of your control, will help you to let go of feelings of guilt.

You may experience anger. Anger must be expressed and shared in a healthy and appropriate manner. Anger occurs mostly when we feel out of control, or we feel resentment towards ourselves or others. Sometimes it's because our personal desires are not fulfilled. When you experience anger, ask yourself, "What is it that I want?" and you will usually find an answer. Anger denies our oneness with all things by placing our desire over what is in our lives. When we get angry, we are trying to take control. Anger clouds our thoughts and keeps us from making calm, sound decisions. If we allow ourselves to approach our feelings of loss in a calm manner, being cognitive (aware) of our reactions and behavior associated with our grief, we can avoid extreme bouts of anger and resentment.

When dealing with grief, increased vulnerability is most likely to manifest. You may feel open and exposed to scrutiny for your feelings. You may feel vulnerable to emotional or physical harm or injury. Feeling weaker and not capable of defending yourself against manipulation, persuasion, or temptation, is a common symptom of one feeling vulnerable.

You will find that grief creates change in almost every phase of life, including social structure. Circumstances often times create changes in our lives. Loss is no exception. Sometimes after a divorce, or break-up, our mutual friends we had as a couple choose to follow one or the other and our social lives change. The friends that your partner brought into the relationship depart with your partner. We find ourselves with some old friends that stay with us and we meet new friends based on our circumstances. Sometimes we lose our in-laws and our spouse's or significant other's relatives, as a result of a death, divorce, break-up, or loss, creating even more loss in our lives.

Less dramatic, but still of considerable mention, is the grief we may experience at the loss of employment. Let's say you lose a job after working for the same company for a long period of time, through attrition or retirement. You may find yourself all of a sudden isolated from your co-workers and workplace friends that you have become accustomed to spending the greater part of your day with. Naturally contact with these individuals decreases and you may find yourself feeling lonely, abandoned, saddened, etc. One or two or even a few of the stages of grief may begin to manifest themselves. Some individuals experiencing this change of employment or status may not have been as attached as others, and may not experience the separation as a loss, but others might. It is important to understand that any loss in our life, no matter how insignificant it may seem to us at the time, can create symptoms of grief.

As we move through the process of grief, we begin to redefine the past, through our thoughts, memories, and reflections. We experience the present through our feelings and emotions, and the circumstances that we find ourselves facing in the moment. As we move forward we begin to create our future and how we define ourselves. As one door closes in our life another begins to open, and as time passes we'll begin again to look for reasons to find purpose, hope, and joy.

In 1969, psychiatrist Elisabeth Kübler-Ross introduced what became known as the "five stages of grief". These stages of grief were based on her studies of the feelings of patients facing terminal illness, but many people have generalized them to other types of negative life changes and losses, such as the death of a loved one or a break-up.

These reactions might not occur in a specific order, and can, at times, occur together. Not everyone experiences all of these emotions:

- Denial, disbelief, numbness
- Anger, blaming others
- Bargaining, for example, "If I am cured of this cancer, I will never smoke again.
- Depressed mood, sadness, and crying
- Acceptance, coming to terms

There are three more types of reactions or behaviors that may occur during the stages of grief, and they can be intertwined within the framework of the five stages mentioned above. They are:

- Numbness (mechanical functioning and social insulation)
- Disorganization (intensely painful feelings of loss)
- Reorganization, i.e., re-entry into a more 'normal' social life.

Both of these lists, and many others, are all descriptive of some of the emotions and functions we go through when we lose a loved one or we suffer a loss, as described previously, and throughout this book.

Grief, like so many other things in our complex lives, can't be reduced to a neat list with absolute definitions, timelines, strategies, goals, and completion dates. If it was that easy, we could freely recognize and work through this stage-by-stage process as if acting in a play, but life is not as simple as that, and circumstances are far more varied than we can anticipate. Grief is as individual as those of us who feel it, and as varied as the circumstances that occur.

Exercise:

- List at least three occasions when something in your life caused you to feel sorrow or grief; it could be the loss of a loved one, a divorce, or separation, or even the loss of a job or social status.

- List how many stages of grief you may have experienced in your past and name them i.e., denial, anger, bargaining, etc.

# ❧ CHAPTER TWO ❧
## Anticipatory Grief

"No one ever told me that grief felt
so like fear."    ~ C.S. Lewis.

## Anticipatory Grief

Anticipatory grief is grief that strikes in advance of an impending loss. You may feel anticipatory grief for a loved one who is sick and dying. Similarly, both children and adults often feel the pain of losses brought on by an upcoming move or divorce. You may feel anticipatory grief for a number of things you feel you have no control over i.e., the pending loss of employment or work reassignment or transfer, a court appearance or pending judicial decision and even in some cases a pending release from being incarcerated, or a change in your environment or personal status. This anticipatory grief helps us prepare for such losses or changes.

Anticipatory grief is very common for anyone watching a loved one succumb to a terminal illness. It is especially common for those who are the primary caregivers of the terminally ill loved one. It is the caregivers who witness death's progression most vividly, and who have little time to reflect on and process their emotions.

Anticipatory grief, like other forms of grief, can invoke a variety of painful thoughts and feelings that are difficult to cope with, which include; depression, extreme concern for the dying person or loss, preparing for the loss, and adjusting to changes caused by the loss. Anticipatory grief gives the family and friends more time to slowly get used to the reality of the loss. In instances of the loss of a loved one or family member, people are able to complete unfinished business with the dying person (for example, saying "good-bye," "I love you," or "I forgive you").

Anticipatory grief may not always occur and does not mean that before the loss, a person feels the same kind of grief as the grief felt after a loss. There is not a set amount of grief that a person will feel. The grief experienced before a death or loss does not make the grief after the death or loss last a shorter amount of time.

Grief that follows an unplanned loss is different from anticipatory grief. Unplanned loss may overwhelm the coping abilities of a person, making normal functioning impossible. Mourners may not be able to realize the total impact of their loss. Even though the person recognizes that the loss occurred, he or she may not be able to accept the loss mentally and emotionally. Following an unexpected loss, the mourner may feel that the world no longer has order and does not make sense.

If you find yourself in the role of being a caregiver, the grieving process can be even more difficult. It is easy for a caregiver to get so busy dealing with everyday activities that they have no room for sadness. There are meals to prepare, perhaps bills to pay, medication to dispense, and so many other activities that must be done, that you find there is no time left for any other activities that you used to do before in your life.

It is possible for all of this grief to build up inside and then at the worst possible moment it all comes rushing to the surface and you aren't able to hold back the sadness. This is not the best way to deal with anticipatory grief.

When caring for a loved one you have to keep going, but it is also important to take care of yourself. Be sure that you find the time to take care of your own needs. Something as simple as your own daily grooming and personal hygiene is very important to be mindful of. Take a "time-out" for a few moments a day to reflect and to work through the emotions you are feeling. Find some time to read a chapter or two of a novel, or write in a journal, write a letter, take a walk, get some fresh air, etc. Talk with understanding groups of friends and relatives. Find someone that can fill in for you for an hour or two a day, to give you some relief and rest, and also to free up some time for yourself.

Some people believe that anticipatory grief is rare. To accept a loved one's death while he or she is still alive may leave the mourner feeling that the dying patient has been abandoned. Expecting the loss often makes the attachment to the dying person stronger.

Although anticipatory grief may help the family, the dying person may experience too much grief, causing the dying person to become withdrawn.  For them, it is a time of facing fears, reflecting on one's life, and saying their good-byes. Even after physical problems are under control by medication or therapy, the dying person faces emotional and perhaps spiritual losses. The thought of leaving the ones they love behind can be an overwhelming emotion and can bring on feelings of helplessness. It is important that the dying person feel your love and willingness to be present. Helping them in a compassionate and loving way to accept and prepare for passing, can provide the nurturing and support that they require during this period of transition.

## Loss of a Child

Children are supposed to outlive their parents, or so we assume. It's a natural assumption in life, but the reality is that accidents, terminal illness, and other factors can take anyone's life, including children, at any time. We don't want to believe this can happen to our children, especially when death happens to an infant, toddler, or young innocent child. When a child's death changes our assumptions about them outliving us, the parents and family members are left with agonizing pain and sorrow, more questions than they have answers for, guilt, denial, anger, (just to name a few of the emotions and feelings associated with grief), and above all a void that is not easily filled in their lives.

When a child is battling a terminal illness and is being cared for in a hospital, nursing facility, or home, the parents and family members naturally become caregivers themselves, caring for the child at bedside, or assisting medical professionals manage in the patient's personal care. The grieving process with many of the stages of grief can be present. Although we can define this type of grief as anticipatory grief, it can be just as painful as a sudden loss and even more difficult.

When a child dies after a long, painful illness and death ends the pain and suffering, the loss is still agonizing, but it may be easier for parents and family members to accept than when death comes accidentally and suddenly to a healthy child. A sudden death of a child, in the case of; Sudden Infant Death Syndrome (SIDS), miscarriage, complications from birth or surgery, accidents, trauma due to crime or natural disasters, and in the event of an older child, suicide or drug overdose, can create for the bereaving, severe grief, leading to complicated or prolonged grief. The grieving process can become even more challenging, and the more severe or heinous the cause of the child's death, the longer and more aggravated the recovery process is likely to be. Complicated and Prolonged Grief is discussed in more detail in the following chapter.

When grieving for the loss of a child, I highly recommend seeking support from a member of your local clergy, rabbi, counselor, or grief professional in your area. Ask for a referral to someone experienced specifically in dealing with grief and recovery from the loss of a child.

## Loss of a Parent

The loss of a parent is the most common form of bereavement in our society.

Parents are expected to die before their children, so it is assumed that we should take the death of a parent in stride. Unfortunately, in our society there is a misgiving that when a parent is middle-aged or elderly that their death is somehow less of a loss than other losses. The real truth is that a parent's death leaves a void in our lives that is in most cases, filled with sadness, yearning, and grief, even when the person was elderly and lived a full life.

If your parent dies after a long period of illness and decline, you may have had time to anticipate their death, but that does not mean that it will make the grieving process any easier, especially if you were the primary caregiver, caring for an elderly parent, and you experienced the daily challenges that the role of caregiver entails. Caring for an elderly parent has its unique set of circumstances and challenges. The parent becomes dependent on your care and with this dependence comes feelings of inadequacy, embarrassment, sadness, guilt, and sometimes depression for the parent. The parent may at first be thankful for your support and relieved, but that can turn to frustration and anger as they struggle to retain their own sense of identity. There is no doubt that both parties are experiencing many of the same emotions that are associated with anticipatory grief. The roles have been reversed. The parent, whom provided the care and needs of the child, now finds himself or herself, feeling vulnerable, and dependent on the adult child, to care for them.

The more significant your relationship is with your parent will determine how you will react to the role of caregiver, and how you and they cope through this period of anticipatory grieving. As stated earlier in this chapter, it is important that your declining parent feel your love and willingness to be present. Helping them in a compassionate and loving way to accept and prepare for passing, can provide the nurturing and support that they require during this period of transition.

Not all of us can be present during this period of parental declining health and transition. If you are an adult child, distanced from your parent that is terminally ill, either geographically, or logistically, then you may experience a different set of emotions than the adult child that is in the caregiver role. You may have feelings of guilt, or frustration, for not being able to attend to their needs. Or you may have obligations that prevent you from participating in the transitional process, that make you feel anxious and unprepared for the inevitable event, when your parent passes. The more significant your relationship was with your parent, the more likely that your reaction to their death will be intense. Grieving is, in part, the cost of emotional commitment. In cases of years of mental or physical abuse by a parent or loved one, the grieving person may also experience feelings of relief, and a sense of peace upon their passing. This may not always be reported, but in some instances these feelings have been expressed by the bereaved. Whatever level of attachment and grief that you may experience, there are sources of support out there to help you cope with and understand your loss.

## Loss of a Pet

For some who've lost an animal companion, the grief and loss can be just as real as losing a human loved one. Our pets live relatively short lives. For many of us who love our pets, their death can affect some of us even more than the death of a relative or friend. The death of a pet leaves few people totally untouched. A pet may come to represent many things to each of us. It may represent a child, or the innocent child in us all. It may reflect the ideal mate or parent. Our pets are faithful, and welcoming, loving us unconditionally. A pet can be a playmate and companion. When a pet dies, we expect that our pain will be acknowledged, even if it is not shared, by our relatives, friends, and colleagues. Most times, we receive very little acknowledgement or sympathy from others. That is just the way it is. The bond between you and your pet is valuable only to you, and represents a personal loss, in most cases. Others generally do not share that same kind of bond as you do, and are not quick to understand your feelings.

Your grief may be compounded by a lack of response from a friend or family member. Realize that you do not need anyone else's approval to mourn the loss of your pet, nor do you have to explain your feelings to anyone. Do not find fault in anyone who cannot appreciate the depth of your grief for a pet. The joy and happiness that you experienced with your pet is a blessing not given to everyone. It is a personal relationship and the loss is a personal one. You can find sympathy and support from other pet owners and people who will understand your feelings and validate your closeness to your pet. You can also get grief counseling for your loss, from animal support and rescue groups. It is hard to understand while mourning the loss of a pet, but your life was and will continue to be brighter because of the time that you shared with your pet. Loss of any kind is a time for emotional healing and growth. Whether your pet dies after battling a long illness, or suddenly through an accident or other cause, the process of grieving for a pet is no different than mourning the death of a human being.

Sudden loss hits you like an explosion, and sends you into shock. But a slow loss arrives more like a glacier, massive and unstoppable, grinding you down. Dealing with an anticipatory grief gets difficult with each passing day. However, there are different ways to overcome and cope with this form of grief, of which some are explained below:

**Crying:** "Don't be afraid to cry. It will free

your mind of sorrowful thoughts." ~ Hopi saying. Holding your tears back or putting on a brave face to look strong for your loved one, family or children will surely be a great emotional support to them but will not likely help you. The extreme emotions that you are experiencing on the inside need to come out. Crying may be the only way you know how to express your grief and sorrow. Do not stop yourself from crying. Crying will give you the emotional release that you need for healing.

**Share Your Feelings:** From our childhood, we have been taught 'sharing is caring', so talk to your friends and share your emotions with them as this will make you feel at peace inside, and the support and love you will get from them will help you to face those tough situations with a stronger and better perception. Talking and sharing with an understanding group of friends or relatives can make all the difference in the world and perhaps bring you comfort in your sorrow.

**Find a Support Group:** You can find a support group, either an organized group of individuals going through the same process, or perhaps a group of caregivers or hospice workers. Check at your local hospital or church group for a referral. Make sure you feel comfortable enough around this group of people to share your feelings, fears, anger, sadness, guilt, etc. There are also several resources on the internet where the members of the group share their thoughts via an online forum. Remember that most of what you discuss over the internet is not always private, so have reservations about giving out any personal information, such as, your address, last name, telephone number, bank account numbers, etc. I remind you of this as a precaution. You may want to remain anonymous while chatting on-line. Having the opportunity to talk and to receive encouragement from others who have been there can make dealing with the grief easier.

**Counseling:** In case you feel shy, reluctant, embarrassed, uncomfortable, or do not want to bother your friends with your personal problems, you can consult a counselor. Explain your situation and the feelings and emotions you are experiencing to a grief counselor. Besides listening and comforting you, the anticipatory grief counseling will also provide you with some effective methods to deal with the grief before and even after the loss.

**Develop New Interests:** Although during the time of grieving, one likes to spend time alone mourning for their loss, the thought of doing something never comes to mind. But, keeping yourself occupied by taking some classes at your local school, college, or adult center, joining a meet-up group of people that share your same interests, i.e., books, hiking, music, etc., or going for daily walks with a couple of friends will definitely help to overcome the pain and sorrow to some extent. Perhaps do some volunteer work in an area or for a cause that interests you.

**Writing in a Diary:** Another way to find relief from your pain, if you choose not to join a support group or share your feelings with others, and a way that may prove to be helpful and simple is to write down your feelings, emotions, fears and uncertainties about life in a diary or journal. You can write it down daily in the form of poetry, short stories, or thoughts and memories. This will help you to know yourself better and how you have come through this crucial, traumatic time with strength and perseverance of not giving up.

Exercise:

- Things that can help me cope with my feelings of loss or anticipatory grief at present.

-  How would you embrace your grief and how would you cope with significant loss in your life?

# ❧ CHAPTER THREE ❧
## Complicated Grief or Prolonged Grief

*"Grief makes one hour ten"*
*~ William Shakespeare*

## Suicide, Addiction, and Sudden Loss

Complicated Grief, now also commonly referred to as Prolonged Grief, can be differentiated from normal grief. Normal grief typically involves a range of transient behaviors and emotional responses to loss. While the experience of grief is a very individual process depending on many factors, certain commonalities are often reported. The normal process of mourning can turn to complicated mourning for a number of reasons. These may include: (a) difficult circumstances surrounding the death, such as multiple losses within a short time period, (b) a person's history of grieving experiences, (c) the personality of the bereaved person, and (d) social factors surrounding the death, such as how the person died and the availability of social support.

Examples of complicated grief can often be found in those who have survived a suicide attempt. Complicated grief responses almost always are a function of intensity and timing; a grief that after a year or two begins to worsen, accompanied by unusual behaviors, is a warning sign. Deaths such as suicides, murders, accidents, and other sudden and unexpected deaths, can result in complicated grief due to the sudden shock. Included in this list could be the stillbirth or miscarriage of a child, sudden infant death syndrome (SIDS), complications due to failed surgery causing the death of a family member or close acquaintance, and death due to natural or man-made disasters.

The surprise makes it difficult to integrate the "story" of the loss, so the person struggles with an initial task of simply believing that the loss has occurred. Variables surrounding the death such as expectedness, naturalness, presence of violence, ambivalence, degree of attachment, and others play into the presence of complicated grief.

Of all the negative experiences we confront in life, probably the hardest to face is the sudden, unexpected loss of someone we love, a family member, or a friend.  Loss in itself is painful enough, but sudden loss can be a great shock to us. The shock doubles our pain and intensifies our grief. When a disaster or an accident occurs which causes death, sudden loss can make the world seem dangerous, unstable, and unsafe to the survivors. This is a natural response to any unexpected and traumatic event.

Sudden loss gives us no chance to prepare. It just happens and we are left in its wake to pick up the pieces and move on with our lives. We can feel cheated, because we did not have a chance to say goodbye to a loved one, or say some final words, express our love with a kiss or a hug, or do one last good thing for that person. We start thinking, "I wish I would have expressed my feeling of affection more often." or "I wish I would have spent more time with that person, perhaps taking a walk or doing some activity one last time." Sudden loss leaves us feeling lost, confused, overwhelmed with pain and sorrow, and even fearful and uncertain. Sudden loss can lead to grief that lasts for weeks, months, or even years. This type of grief we define as complicated or prolonged grief.

All too often, complicated grief can last for years and most people such as friends, colleagues, and acquaintances, and even family members of the mourner, will withdraw from the mourner when hearing that this sort of grief may still be present after several years. The mourner's prolonged grief can have an adverse affect on the other family members. It can cause stress and anxiety for the children, and in the case of a spouse that is unable to cope with the mourner's complicated grief, in some cases may result in further loss through separation or divorce.

Mourners may risk withdrawal themselves. This can lead to depression and further disassociation. It is important for the bereaving person to remain active in daily family activities and discussions, as well as, remain active in his or her community, church, school, support, and peer group.

For the loved one, family member, or friend of the person grieving, it can be difficult to know what to say or do, especially when it comes to complicated or prolonged grief. It's common to feel awkward, helpless or unsure. You may feel uncomfortable or afraid of intruding, saying the wrong thing, or making things worse. It is perfectly acceptable to offer your condolences, and express your concern for the welfare of the mourner. You may offer your support and express your desire to help in some way. Even running a few errands, or helping them with things around the house, taking them to lunch, or grocery shopping with them or for them are ways that you can show your support.

Show the person that you care about their situation, and above all be honest and genuine in your statements. It is important to have patience with the individual and be a good listener. Don't push the mourner into discussing their feeling if they are not ready to open up to discuss them with you. If they are willing to discuss their feeling, let them. Offer them comfort and reassurance. If they are experiencing symptoms of severe depression or they express suicidal thoughts or behaviors, perhaps you can encourage them in a calm and caring manner to seek counseling for their depression and feelings of grief. This may be all the person needs to hear from someone else to help them make the decision to seek help. If you sense that the mourner is in imminent danger of doing harm to his or herself, or is unable to care for his or herself as result of their depression, then you should by all means take appropriate action, by notifying the proper authorities or professionals, that are qualified to deal with extreme cases of depression, suicide, or addiction, and who can intervene and prevent further physical or emotional harm to the individual experiencing complicated grief.

While it's not known specifically what causes complicated grief, researchers continue to learn more about the factors that may increase the risk of developing it. These risk factors may include:

- An unexpected or violent death
- Suicide of a loved one
- Lack of a support system or friendships
- Traumatic childhood experiences, such as abuse or neglect
- Childhood separation anxiety
- Close or dependent relationship to the deceased person
- Being unprepared for the death

- In the case of a child's death, the number of remaining children
- Lack of resilience or adaptability to life changes

Complicated grief can affect you physically, mentally and socially. Without appropriate treatment, these complications can include:
- Depression
- Suicidal thoughts or behaviors
- Increased risk of heart disease, cancer and high blood pressure
- Anxiety
- Long-term impairment in daily living
- Post-traumatic stress disorder
- Substance abuse
- Smoking or nicotine use

In addition, complicated grief can cause nightmares, appetite problems, dryness of mouth, shortness of breath, and sleep disorders to name just a few of the symptoms that can manifest. Repetitive motions to avoid pain are often reported by people experiencing normal grief. Even visions or hallucinatory experiences may be normal early in the grieving process.

There is a clinical problem of becoming "identified" with the grief.  In this situation, mourners are reluctant to release the grief because grieving has been integrated as part of their identity. Scientists suggest that complicated grief activates neurons in the reward centers of the brain, possibly giving these memories addiction-like properties.

Exercise:

- List at least three reasons why the normal process of grieving can turn to complicated grieving.

# ✎ CHAPTER FOUR ✎
## Grief and Suicide

"Tell me, how can I live without my Husband any longer? This is my first awakening thought each morning, and as I watch the waves of the turbulent lake under our windows I sometimes feel I should like to go under them." ~ Mary Ann Todd Lincoln

## Grief and Suicide

We all feel overwhelmed by difficult emotions or situations sometimes. But most people get through it, or can put their problems in perspective and find a way to carry on with determination and hope. So why does one person attempt suicide when another person in the same tough situation does not? What makes some people more resilient (better able to deal with life's setbacks and difficulties) than others? What makes a person unable to see another way out of a bad situation besides ending his or her life?

The answer to those questions lies in the fact that most people who commit suicide have depression. Loss can lead to depression, and depression leads people to focus mostly on failures and disappointments, to emphasize the negative side of their situations, and to downplay their own capabilities or worth. Someone with severe depression is unable to see the possibility of a good outcome and may believe they will never be happy or things will never go right for them again.

Depression affects a person's thoughts in such a way that the person doesn't see when a problem can be overcome. The loss of a loved one or a way of life can seem overwhelming and the loss can create panic, anxiety, and depression. It's as if the depression puts a filter on the person's thinking that distorts things. That's why depressed people don't realize that suicide is a permanent solution to a temporary problem in the same way that other people do. A person with depression may feel like there's no other way out of problems, no other escape from emotional pain, or no other way to communicate their desperate unhappiness. Sometimes people who feel suicidal may not even realize they are depressed. They are unaware that it is the depression, and not the situation, that's influencing them to see things in a "there's no way out," "it will never get better," "there's nothing I can do" kind of way.

When depression lifts because a person gets the proper therapy or treatment, the distorted thinking is cleared. The person can find pleasure, energy, and hope again. But while someone is seriously depressed, suicidal thinking is a real concern.

A person can also experience grief from their attempt at suicide. The feeling of loss of their way of life and perspective, as well as feeling loss of their identity and failure after the suicide attempt can lead to further depression. It is important to realize that suicidal thoughts are just that, thoughts, and should not be acted on. When we realize this we can redirect these negative thoughts and insert a wedge in their place. For example, if we realize that these suicidal thoughts are just a product of our thinking and not concrete, or based in reality, and that there are alternative thoughts of a positive nature that we can entertain, we can redirect our thoughts to other more reasonable and constructive solutions to our situation or circumstances.

If we realize that we are grieving and we are depressed, and that these thoughts are a product of that process, we can understand that this is just a stage we are going through and we do not have to act on it. If we understand the stages of grief and grieving, as we learn and as discussed in chapter one, we can navigate through these feelings and not make suicide a permanent solution to a temporary problem or situation.

If you have been thinking about suicide, get help now. Depression is powerful. You can't wait and hope that your mood might improve. When a person has been feeling down for a long time, it's hard to step back and be objective. Talk to someone you trust as soon as you can. Talk to a counselor, talk to a coach, a teacher, a relative, a member of the clergy, rabbi, or chaplain, and get the support that you need.

Exercise:

- Think of a situation where you felt overwhelmed by grief or loss and may have had suicidal thoughts. What did you do to get past those thoughts?

- If you did not have suicidal thoughts, explain why you did not. Example: religious beliefs, support group, family, friends, responsibilities, your children, etc.

- Think of some coping techniques that you could use in the event that you become depressed and feel suicidal or the need to turn to drugs or alcohol:

# ❧ CHAPTER FIVE ❧
## Grief and Addiction

"What is out of sight disturbs men's minds
more seriously than what they see."
~ Julius Caesar

## Grief and Addiction

Grief is not a place people like to stay in for long. It hurts, it just plain hurts. And who wants that? But anytime you try to think about this person who was in your life or in your memories, you can't help but face the reality that they are gone from your life now. If you think about a situation or a way of life that has changed, you can't help but feel a loss of what was. Doing that means consciously revisiting pain. If you have an addiction or addictive tendencies, it's very likely you will be tempted to escape the pain and reality through the use of alcohol or drugs.

An addiction is a temporary fix turned into a bad habit. Drugs and alcohol will cover or distort your feelings of grief for a while, but eventually they create a bigger problem than they solve. Not only does a drug or alcohol addiction cut you off from being aware of your emotions; it pushes the grieving process out in front of you longer. In other words, it doesn't let you skip your grieving, but rather puts it on hold until you face your emotions more honestly, and then you get to go through the grieving process for real. Otherwise, you are completely shutting off your grief any time it gets close to the surface.

However, a person with an alcohol or drug addiction often ends up hurting their body with the chemicals they ingest or inject. If you already have a mental illness such as Bipolar Disorder or intense anxiety, adding grief to the mix can really crank up your addiction. If you have been sober for some time when your grief hits, you are at a serious risk for addiction relapse. The only way to really cope with your grief is to face it and learn how to live with it. The empty place in your heart may never go away, but the terrible sting can be softened, making your loss something you can put aside when you need to, and visit for periods of time if you want. This takes time and emotional honesty. You can't be emotionally honest with yourself or anyone else if you have an active addiction.

Getting into a drug rehab program can help break the addictive behaviors and can get you back on the right track in your grieving process.

Another form of grief can be experienced when we kick a long-term addiction. For an addict in recovery, there is a period of grief that occurs when leaving their old way of life. This feeling is a normal part of any major change in life, but is often misunderstood during the process of recovery. This grief creates quite a conflict within the addict. They are being pulled in two opposite directions, one that says freedom from active addiction is absolutely desirable, and a second that keeps reminding them how good the addictive behavior felt. It can be difficult for someone in recovery to admit they miss parts of their addiction and the lifestyle it created. It can be equally difficult for someone who has not had an addiction to wrap their mind around why someone would miss something so bad for them.

In the interactions between the addict and those who are supporting them in their program, this withdrawal from addiction grief can cause misunderstanding. It is important to recognize this grieving process as a normal part of recovery. It in no way indicates how successful an individual will be in achieving long-term abstinence from their addiction. Just as with grief in other areas of life, each individual will experience a different mixture of feelings as they realize they will never again get to partake in their favored activity, and that they will miss it. By refusing to acknowledge and openly discuss these feelings, an environment of isolation and shame is created for the addict. This grieving process needs to be accepted as part of being human.

The way human memory works is interesting. We tend to remember the good parts of a situation, while the bad parts fade. In some instances, this way of remembering works for us. If we remembered how horrible or painful some experiences we had were, then very few women would have a second child, and hardly anyone would move a second time. This type of memory function can also work against us, especially when it involves something that caused us harm, but also had enjoyable parts. We forget the hangovers and remember all the parties. Making a frustrating situation even harder is that using is the addict's most used coping skill. The addiction is no longer a viable option for much needed soothing. They are experiencing all this stress and change and may not yet have a healthy way to deal with everything. This creates a situation where a person longs for the comfort of their addiction. An addict is susceptible to thoughts of using at this point. It is a knee-jerk reaction to say, "If it's going to suck this much then why am I even bothering?" Things generally calm down as new coping skills are found and the hard work begins to get results, but this is a process and it does take time.

Knowing the substance or behavior has become unhealthy does not erase the fact that at some point it was fun and comforting, and having to put it down is still a loss on some level. Grieving is a necessary process for accepting any loss or change. While some may feel that no longer participating in an addiction is in no way comparable to losing a loved one, there are many addicts who would disagree. A person must be allowed to grieve the loss of things that are important to them, whether those things were good for them or not, and addiction is no exception.

As you can see, grief can take on many forms and also cause us to have destructive thoughts that can lead us to make poor choices. Whether it is the thought of taking our lives to end our despair or our overwhelming feelings of helplessness, or thoughts of easing the pain through the use of alcohol or drugs, these actions can result in terrible consequences not only to ourselves, but to the loved ones and the people around us, especially causing them to experience the same, if not worse, grief than we are experiencing. Ask yourself, would you want your children or loved ones to suffer that kind of grief because of your actions?    By understanding the grieving process and the stages that we experience during it, and recognizing the symptoms and the warning signs, we can be better prepared to embrace our emotions and allow ourselves to grieve in less destructive ways.

Remember that negative thoughts are just a product of our thinking and are not concrete or based in reality, and that there are alternative thoughts of a positive nature that we can entertain. We can redirect our thoughts to other more reasonable and constructive solutions to our situation or circumstances. You do not have to turn your negative thoughts into negative actions or addictions.

Exercise:

- If during the grieving process you became addicted to drugs or alcohol, what are some of the positive constructive things you could do to fill the empty void that drugs and alcohol filled during your addiction?

# ❧ CHAPTER SIX ❧
## Grief and Sudden Loss

"It is not the strongest of the species that survives, nor the most intelligent that survives. It is the one that is the most adaptable to change."
~ Charles Darwin

## Sudden Loss

A sudden, accidental, unexpected or traumatic loss shatters the world as we know it. It is often a loss that does not make sense. We realize that life is not always fair and that sometimes bad things happen to good people. The sudden loss leaves us feeling shaken, unsure and vulnerable. A sudden loss is one that occurs without any notice. A traumatic loss is one that is sudden, violent, disfiguring, or destructive. It can be caused by a natural event that is random, or a deliberate event, that can involve the loss of multiple lives. It can also be an event in which the mourner has a personal encounter with death.

Loss and death due to a sudden or traumatic accident or disaster can create complex issues for the survivors. The grief process is often very different from an expected or anticipated death. Sudden loss due to a tragic event can cause Post Traumatic Stress Disorder (PTSD), as well as, many other complex and diverse emotional, physical, and psychological problems for the survivors and their families.

Examples of sudden and tragic loss can be the result of; heart attacks, strokes, aneurisms, accidents, failed surgical procedures, all resulting in death. Other examples include; Sudden Infant Death Syndrome (SIDS), murder, suicide, natural disasters, such as, earthquakes, floods, tornadoes, hurricanes, tsunamis, and human caused events, such as, war, terrorist attacks, and global or regional civil uprisings. There are many causes and events that can result in the unanticipated loss of life, accidents and sudden illness being two of the most common causes. Tragedy can strike at any time, and when it does, the survivors are left in the wake of the tragedy to pick up the pieces of their lives, rebuild and move on.

Grief from a sudden or traumatic loss can be devastating and this type of grief can easily develop into complicated and prolonged grief. The survivor should be aware of the dynamic symptoms and affects this type of loss can have on them. As with any loss, many of the stages of grief and grieving that we have discussed in the previous chapters can be present. Due to the nature of the sudden and unexpected traumatic loss or event, these stages of grief can manifest themselves in a more complex manner.

## Natural Disasters

Natural disasters, such as, earthquakes, floods, tornadoes, hurricanes, droughts, and tsunamis can create traumatic losses of life, property, and valuables. Multiple deaths can occur during one or a combination of these events. A sudden tragic event shatters our sense of order and thrusts us into a world forever changed. Survivors of a natural disaster may experience a greater sense of vulnerability and heightened anxiety. The safe world we once knew, no longer exists. We fear for ourselves, our family and friends. Survivors can become overwhelmingly preoccupied with thoughts that such a random act of a violent nature might happen again. Not only are the survivors faced with the task of rebuilding their homes, and lives, but they may have loss of employment, social networking, and support services. The whole foundation of their world is shaken and grieving may take a back seat to survival.

However, the initial feelings of fear, shock and disbelief will give way to feeling of sadness, yearning and grief. Depression may set in sooner and stronger under these circumstances and the desire not to live and face what seems to be insurmountable odds may set in. Eventually the will to live will take over, but it is important that the survivors discuss these feelings of depression and grief with trauma or triage professionals if they are available, or with family members and fellow survivors. It takes time to reorganize after a natural disaster, but eventually things will get back to a somewhat normal pace. Change occurs often throughout our lives and the ability to adapt is a part of life. Remember to have patience and realize that change is possible and the feelings you are experiencing are part of the grief and grieving process.

## Man-made Disasters

Man-made disasters, such as, the terrorist attack on the World Trade Center on September 11th, hijackings, or bombings, are considered random acts of violence and can be more frightening than natural disasters. Declarations of war, although considered planned by one government, against the other, and the subsequent loss of lives that result, are still considered man-made acts committed by human beings. These acts are not considered "acts of God", as natural disasters are perceived. Man-made disasters, as well as natural disasters, create traumatic loss of life and result in the survivors experiencing grief and grieving.

There are differences between man-made disasters and natural disasters that make man-made disasters, especially a terrorist attack more stressful and sudden. There is no prior warning; therefore there is no time to prepare. Unlike a forecast hurricane or the rising of flood waters, there is no time to get ready, move inland, or to higher ground. The man-made terrorist attack just happens, leaving the survivors in shock, confused, and in disbelief.

It is difficult to comprehend how any one individual or any group could carefully and deliberately cause so much death, destruction, and injuries. Terrorist acts can lead us to question our fundamental beliefs and values. It causes confusion, making us feel unsure, unsafe, and fearful. Unless we are able to protect ourselves, our families, and our way of life, we become more and more insecure, and less trustful of our neighbors, and strangers. We lose faith in our civil and government officials and military personnel's capability of protecting us, and therefore, lose hope and direction in our lives. This frustration and fear leads to further isolation, grief, and grieving, and can result in a breakdown of our family unit, and social communities. At times of extreme and sudden loss, it is important to understand the forces that are at play, and remain cognizant (aware) of all of our emotional responses to the circumstances.

## War and Loss

As discussed earlier in this chapter, declarations of war, although considered planned by one government, against the other, and certainly when executed, always results in loss of lives. War is considered a man-made act committed by human beings. Usually both sides of the conflict experience loss. There may be a considerable amount of anticipatory grief associated with war, as generals and soldiers alike, prepare to do battle and sacrifice their lives for a cause. Civilian lives lost and collateral damage can occur as well. This loss of lives can happen suddenly and without warning. No government planning or evacuation of cities or communities can completely guarantee the safety of its citizens in a time of war. The scenario of conflict will create grief and grieving for not only anticipation of loss, but for sudden loss, and the aftermath of any war leaves devastation in its wake.

Both soldiers and citizens can experience Post Traumatic Stress Disorder (PSTD), as governments, communities, and families rebuild themselves. The trauma and horror of war can leave permanent physical and mental scars, but with the help of medical and psychological professionals, counselors, as well as, support from family members, clergy, and the community, survivors can regain hope and go on to lead productive and purposeful lives.

Exercise:

- How would you cope with sudden loss in your life?

- How would you help others cope during a traumatic event or crisis?

# ᖇ CHAPTER SEVEN ᖈ
## Coping with Grief and Grieving

"How indeed" "He copes, like everybody
else, as well as he can, that's all. And it's
usually deplorably enough."
~ Carl Gustav Jung

## Coping with Grief and Grieving

Coping is a normal part of living with a
loss. It is the struggle you go through every
day to meet your own needs and the demands
of your new situation. The struggle is to cope
well, rather than in unhealthy and destructive
ways. Coping in a good way might include
maintaining your faith, finding value in being
around others, or just doing better than you
did yesterday. Everyone reacts differently to
loss. It is important to find ways to cope that
will work for you. Consider the following
ideas for managing the grief process:

- Embrace gentleness. Your body and
  soul need repair. Give your body rest.
  When possible, go to bed earlier.

- Accept help when offered and seek help if a problem is unresolved.
- Get together with other people. Join talk groups and attend self-help or vocational classes.
- Speak with a counselor, chaplain, rabbi, or a member of the clergy.
- Focusing on others will help you deal with the pain.
- Holidays and special occasions are difficult, so discuss your feelings with a peer coach, counselor, chaplain, rabbi, or a member of the clergy, during these times for support.
- Be patient. If you feel minor depression for a while, it is okay.
- Look for comforting activities. Learn to express your feelings, talk, write, sing, exercise, and cry.
- Learn more about grief recovery. A greater understanding helps us cope.
- Good nutrition is important. Avoid junk food.
- Do something for someone else.
- Find, strengthen, or reestablish your spirituality.
- Meditate.

Relaxation techniques such as muscle relaxation, concentrated breathing, and meditation can teach you how to relax. By allowing yourself to relax you will find it much easier to cope physically, mentally, and spiritually with your feelings of grief and grieving. The key is regular practice. Try to set aside at least 30 minutes a day. Over time, the relaxation response will come easier and easier, until it feels natural.

- Muscle and body relaxation. When grief takes hold and you feel sad, worried, anxious, or fearful, muscle and body relaxation can help you release muscle tension and take a "time out" from your worries. The technique involves systematically tensing and then releasing different muscle groups in your body. A form of isometric exercising, muscle tension and then muscle release exercises will not only build muscle groups, but also can help in the relaxation process if done properly. As your body relaxes, your mind will follow.

- Concentrated breathing. When you're anxious, you breathe faster. This hyperventilation causes symptoms such as dizziness, shortness of breath, lightheadedness, increased heart rate, and possible numbness in your hands and feet. These physical symptoms are frightening, leading to further anxiety and fear. But concentrating on your breathing, taking notice as your stomach expands, as you breathe in clean oxygen, breathing from your diaphragm, and exhaling through your mouth or nose as you watch your stomach contract, and then gently repeating the process, you can reverse these symptoms and calm yourself down. You can also practice quiet breathing; by slowly breathing in to the count of three and holding it for a count of three and then exhaling to the count of three. It takes some practice, but after several tries you will see how easy it is to be aware of and control your breathing.

- Meditation. Many types of meditation have been shown to reduce anxiety.

Meditation allows the practitioner to train his or her mind through self-awareness to induce an altered state of consciousness in order to realize some benefit. In many research studies, various methods of meditation have been linked to changes in metabolism, blood pressure, brain activation, and other bodily processes. Meditation has been used in clinical settings as a method of stress and pain reduction. Research shows that meditation can actually change your brain. With regular practice, meditation boosts activity on the left side of the prefrontal cortex, the area of the brain responsible for feelings of serenity, comfort, and joy.

## Coping Exercises

These brief exercises can be useful to help you cope with grief:

## Falling Leaf

Instructions: Stare at a spot on the wall across from you. Visualize a leaf on that spot. With each breath, count backward from 20 to 1 as you watch the leaf very slowly drift to the ground. At 1, the leaf reaches the ground and you are deeply relaxed.

## Affirmation
**I will find my sources**
**of support and use them.**

## Self-Awareness

Now is a good time to ask, "What really comforts me?" Family and friends may have good intentions about what is helpful, but you need to decide what is best for you. Care for your own needs first. Your body, mind, and spirit are a team. Allow them to work together and try not to ignore any area.

You may find a need to deepen your faith, since spirituality can be a source of hope and comfort for some people. Counseling may be a healthy choice for some people. Take it as a sign of good health if you choose to get involved with counseling and/or a support group. Remember: The most loving thing you can give to the one you lost or to yourself when you experience loss is being true to yourself.

## Meditation

Just relax and make yourself comfortable sitting or lying in a relaxed position, with your eyes open or closed, begin by becoming aware of your breath.

Feel your breath as it enters with a cool feeling and then warming as it gently travels down into your lungs.

Fill your lungs with clean oxygen, bringing in energy, vitality and healing energy.

As you exhale, feel your body releasing toxins, stress, anxiety, and any negative thoughts or feelings that have accumulated.

Stay with this breath, focusing on the feeling of deep peace for a few more easy inhalations and exhalations.

Feel the warm healing energy that runs through the body and become aware of the warmth and tingling of every cell.

Feel the energy that is in the extended environment, out to infinity, in the entire cosmos, in every part of nature and in every living thing and bring all those energies together and feel them as one.

Visualize all of that energy shining brightly and creating healing warmth and allow it to flow through your body, from the tip of your head all the way down to the tips of your toes.

Your whole body is now filled with Divine Healing Light and Energy. Feel it warming, healing and expanding.

Feel yourself opening up to this energy as you let go of your feelings of sadness and loss.

Allow yourself to experience a moment of peace, joy and happiness, as you think and remember only happy memories and thoughts.

Now bring your thoughts into the present moment and feel the calmness and relaxation as it sweeps over your whole body.

Bring your awareness to any intentions or desires that you may have and hold the thoughts of those intentions or desires as you allow the Healing Energy to bring your deepest hopes and wishes to life and your intentions into reality.

Allow yourself to believe that you can live through and beyond this moment in time and that the pain that you have been experiencing will subside, just as it has while experiencing this moment of safeness, contentment, and peace.

All the grief and grieving will be replaced with understanding and peace of mind, allowing you to once again find happiness and joy in life.

Know that you can return to this healing place of peace and tranquility, any time that you desire, by using this method for easy relaxation.

Each time that you use this meditation, you will relax more easily, more quickly, and more deeply.

So now  take one last deep breath in and then exhale feeling calm, secure, confident, in control, and empowered to make good choices as you go about your daily activities.

Exercise:

- Things that will help me cope right now. Make a list:

# ❧ CHAPTER EIGHT ❧
## Managing Sadness and Yearning

"Tears are the silent language of grief."
~ Voltaire

## Sadness and Yearning

The Encarta Dictionary defines sadness as a noun used to describe a feeling of, or showing, unhappiness, grief, or sorrow. In the same text it describes yearning as a strong desire, often tinged with sadness. Loss can trigger profound sadness. Profound sadness is probably the most universally experienced symptom of grief. You may have feelings of emptiness, despair, yearning, or deep loneliness. You may also cry a lot or feel emotionally unstable. Sadness can affect our thinking, as well as our mood and body. Indications of unhappiness include losing interest in pleasurable activities and hobbies, difficulty concentrating, remembering, and making decisions. Although sadness and depression have many similar symptoms, they are not the same. It is important not to confuse signs of sadness with symptoms of depression. Depression is also a stage of the grief and grieving process, and depending on the severity of the depression, can result in experiencing similar emotions and feelings as with sadness. More severe depression can be the result of complicated grief, which we discussed in chapter three, and can manifest itself at any time, if not observed and corrected, and could very well lead to addiction or suicide. If you are feeling depressed, it is important to seek out the advice and care of a professional therapist, medical doctor, or psychologist. For the purposes of our discussion in this chapter we are concentrating on the causes and symptoms of sadness and yearning due to a loss.

Feelings of sadness can come in waves. These waves of emotions of sadness and yearning can come and go, and the intensity varies considerably. Just when we feel that things are finally getting easier to cope with, something can unexpectedly trigger a whole new flood of feelings. Allow yourself to roll with the tides of these emotions and feelings, being aware that this is all part of the healing process.

Sadness and yearning for a loved one, an object, or a way of life you have lost are the most common and expected feelings that occur after any loss. Although sadness and yearning may always be present, and the grieving person may continue to miss the deceased person for many years, perhaps a lifetime, life goes on and the grieving person will move on with their life.

One of the best things you can do to cope with your sadness and yearning is to talk to someone or write in a journal about how you feel. Sharing your feelings with people who care about you can help alleviate some of the sadness.

Other steps you can take to cope with your feelings of sadness and yearning include:

- Looking at pictures and photos, watching home movies, or discussing with other people things you remember about the person or subject of your loss.

- Taking part in activities that acknowledge a loss, such as, attending a funeral or memorial services after a death. If you cannot do this, because you cannot travel or you are incapacitated, then do this in your mind and know that as you visit this activity in your thoughts, you are finding closure. You can imagine going to a going-away party for a friend or even for a former lifestyle, etc.

- Take care of yourself and keep yourself healthy. Try to keep a regular schedule and maintain the basics of good health. Exercise, eat healthy and nutritious foods, and get plenty of rest. You may need more rest than usual. This is the time to be good to yourself. Take a walk, listen to music, get your hair styled, or maybe get a massage.

- Don't be afraid to go out and have some fun. When you are sad, humor and laughter can be a great remedy for the heart and the spirit. It is not a betrayal of the loved one to be able to feel some joy.

- Avoid unrealistic expectations of yourself. Grieving takes time and energy, so pace yourself. Don't take on more than you can handle to the point of feeling overwhelmed.

- Participate in normal day-to-day activities. Taking part in daily activities keeps you focused in the present.

Although it may seem that your feelings of sadness and yearning will last a long time, remind yourself that these feelings will lessen and perhaps even eventually subside as time goes by.

Exercise:

- How would you cope when experiencing the following emotions during the grieving process? Sadness and Yearning.

# ❧ CHAPTER NINE ❧
## Managing Worry and Anxiety

"Some of your hurts you have cured,
and the sharpest you still have survived,
but what torments of grief you endured
from the evil which never arrived."
~ Ralph Waldo Emerson

## Worry and Anxiety

Some researchers say that "It's normal to worry from time to time". Our life paths have many unknowns and challenges, and worry could be considered a very natural response to many situations. Worrying can be helpful when it motivates you to take action and solve a problem. But if you're preoccupied with "what ifs" and "worst-case scenarios", worry becomes a problem of its own. Worry can also be very troublesome and interfere with our ability to function freely and calmly in our daily lives. More importantly, it can lead to fear and anxiety and make our journey through the grief and grieving process more difficult. Too much worry can distract you from important matters and prevent you from thinking clearly. Worry can make you anxious and anxiety can become fear. Fear can consume your thoughts and prevent you from moving forward in a clear and concentrated effort. Fear can inhibit action or problem solving. We can find ourselves locked in an internal battle with ourselves, unable to break through this barrier of anxiety and fear. We can become paralyzed with worry and become unable to focus on, or implement, constructive solutions to our problems.

Sometimes in our grief and grieving we may find ourselves consistently worrying about the future. We start to imagine future failures, dangers or other types of negative outcomes, which may or may not exist, but in our minds seem very real. We become locked in this internal struggle to make sense of our loss or losses. We may ruminate, or repeat in our mind, the same worry or worries, and try to stop worrying by anxious avoidance of certain situations. Our thoughts of worry, anxiety, fear, and failure can become a self-fulfilling prophesy. But we do not have to allow this to happen. Becoming cognizant (aware) of the processes taking place in our minds, and realizing that these thought processes are all a part of the grief and grieving process, can help us to calm down and control our thoughts and behaviors, allowing us to navigate through all of these thoughts and emotions, more at ease with ourselves, and better prepared to cope with situations and our emotions.

You can manage your worry and anxiety by:

- Talking or writing about the things that are bothering you. Even if you are not sure what is bothering you, finding words for your feelings often helps you figure out what is causing your anxiety.

- Taking charge of whatever you can. Making plans to deal with your concerns helps relieve the worry and anxiety and sense of insecurity. Resist the urge to make major life decisions when you are anxious or worried.

- Allow other people to do some things for you that you would normally do yourself. If worries and concerns are preventing you from taking care of personal needs, tasks, and other responsibilities, ask for help. Allowing other people to help you also helps them. It gives them an opportunity to show they care.

- Ask for emotional support and companionship until you feel less anxious and worried. Ask someone you trust to stay with you. This is not a sign of weakness.

- Exercising has a way of making us feel better. When you exercise you will be giving your mind a break from the worries and anxiety that have been consuming your thoughts. You will also be releasing chemicals within your body that work to improve your overall health and well being.

- Meditation and relaxation have been proven to reduce worry and stress. Try to set some time aside each day to meditate or relax in your favorite place, or in your favorite chair. Perhaps take a nice warm bath, while listening to soothing music. Perhaps relax by reading a book, or gardening.

By using any or all of the suggestions above, you will begin to see positive results, managing worry and anxiety, as you navigate through the grief and grieving process, leading to a more balanced life.

Exercise:

- How would you cope when experiencing the following emotions during the grieving process? Worry and anxiety.

# ❧ CHAPTER TEN ❧
## Managing Feelings of Guilt

*"But they whose guilt within their bosoms lie,
imagine every eye beholds their blame"
~ William Shakespeare*

## Feelings of Guilt

According to the Encyclopedia of Psychology, 2nd edition 2001, "Guilt is a cognitive or an emotional experience that occurs when a person realizes or believes—accurately or not—that he or she has violated a moral standard, and bears significant responsibility for that violation. It is closely related to the concept of remorse". You may ask, "What does this have to do with the grief and grieving process?"

When a loved one dies, feelings of guilt are normal. We may blame ourselves for something we did or didn't do that may have contributed to the death, or for things that we wish we did or didn't say or do. This is fairly common. Some people, however, become tortured by their feelings of guilt and it affects their whole life. Guilt is a strong emotion which is often magnified because when we experience the loss of a loved one, or someone close to us, we are in an extremely vulnerable state. The guilt is often experienced when we try to answer the unanswerable: "Why did my loved one have to die?" or "Why did they leave me?"

Most people going through the grieving process feel some degree of guilt. None of us can live close to another person and love deeply without hurting that person. We all do and say things we later regret. We know these things hurt our loved one. When a loved one has died, or has left us physically, we are reminded of those hurts and failings, real or imagined. We are reminded of words we regret saying, incidents we'd like to forget, actions we'd like to take back. We consider every possible action that we could have taken or not taken to prevent the death.

Guilt is usually not satisfied with explanations. Often we feel helpless with our guilt because there is little that we can do to correct the situation. A direct personal relationship is desired to take away the guilt, or to ask forgiveness, but that is not possible because our loved one is physically gone. When we feel guilty justifiably and we are unable to be forgiven directly by the deceased or person that is no longer with us, we may find some relief by talking with a trusted friend about our feelings of guilt. It is important to find a friend who will listen and be accepting of our feelings, without being judgmental.

Feelings of guilt, which are common in all grief, are often of major concern among survivors whose loved ones have died by suicide. "Could I have prevented it?" "Is it my fault?" "How did I fail?" Most survivors say that their grief was complicated by extreme feelings of guilt. For some, the guilt never goes away. Either they let it ruin their lives, or they allow it to diminish to the point where they can handle it.

It is important for you to accept your guilt, however illogical, to understand it and to deal with it. It's unhealthy and even damaging to stay with guilt feelings. It may take great effort but it is worth such effort because guilt that is unrecognized or unresolved for a long period may lead to illnesses both mental and physical, brought on by anxiety and despair, and to years of unhappiness. Remember, we can't change the past. There is so much pain in grief that it is not helpful to continue to blame and accuse ourselves. If your guilt is too overwhelming or preventing you from moving on with your life, seek professional counseling. Don't be afraid or embarrassed to talk about your feelings of guilt with those who have been trained to help.

If you find yourself feeling guilty about a past action or inaction, set aside time to think about your feelings and work through the following exercises:

- Write a list of your "should haves" and "shouldn't haves."

- Think about how you would have done things differently.

- Think about anything you can do to help someone or thank someone that you may have not properly thanked in the past.  Forgive yourself for those regrets that you cannot act on to correct.

- Recognize the things that you have done right and where you have been successful. This may help you put things in better perspective.

- Be kind and gentle with yourself during this exercise. If you look back on something in your past, you can usually see the situation more clearly and think of a better way to handle it. Remind yourself that you did the best you could at the time.

Exercise:

- How would you cope when experiencing the following emotions during the grieving process? Feelings of Guilt.

# ✎ CHAPTER ELEVEN ✎
## Managing Frustration and Anger

"To spare oneself from grief at all costs
can be achieved only at the price of
total detachment, which excludes the
ability to experience happiness."
~ Erich Fromme

## Frustration and Anger

Frustration is a common emotional response to opposition. Related to anger and disappointment, it arises from the perceived resistance to the fulfillment of individual will. The greater the obstruction, and the greater the will, the more the frustration is likely to be. Causes of frustration may be internal or external. In people, internal frustration may arise from challenges in fulfilling personal goals and desires, instinctual drives and needs, or dealing with perceived deficiencies, such as a lack of confidence or fear of social situations.

Anger is an emotion related to one's psychological interpretation of having been offended, wronged or denied and a tendency to undo that by retaliation. Anger has also been described as a normal emotion that involves a strong, uncomfortable, and emotional response to a perceived provocation.

To someone experiencing grief and grieving, the emotions of frustration at first, and then frustration turning to anger, can usually be attributed to external factors that are beyond his or her control. The loss of a loved one or someone close to the individual can trigger feelings of helplessness and frustration. Loss can also bring on feelings of responsibility for not being able to prevent the loss in some way, or feelings of anger towards someone else for not preventing the loss. In some cases, you may feel anger towards the individual that has died or is no longer with you, for leaving you. This can also lead to feelings of anger in one's self or guilt.

You may struggle with these feelings of frustration and anger related to loss, and you might try to hide your feelings in the hope that they will disappear. Unfortunately, intense feelings must be recognized and dealt with; they don't just disappear on their own.

You may become angry and blame others for what has happened, even though it is not their fault. This is called displaced anger. You may get angry with a higher power, such as God. Frustration and anger can affect people emotionally and physically.

Anger and frustration at having to deal with challenges while caring for an individual who is sick or dying, or who is in a hospice situation, especially when that person is close to you is part of the process of anticipatory grief and grieving. It is part of the emotional process. You may ask yourself, "Why me?!" That's a common reaction to any challenge. Why not? Everyone has problems and challenges, and you are no exception. That's the hard truth. It's amazing, though, how the challenges you face can make you a much stronger person if you choose to move beyond them.

You can work out these feelings by talking with someone or through physical activity, such as walking, concentrated breathing, yoga, exercise, cleaning, or even in some cases punching a pillow. Working out frustration and anger in a physical way, such as exercise, helps relieve muscle tension and may reduce restlessness and irritation. Never take out your anger on another human being or animal. Unresolved frustration and anger may grow until you are not able to deal with them. You may then yell, scream, or hit someone or something. This is not good!! It is never acceptable to hit another human being or animal!! Unexpressed frustration and anger can also cause other problems, such as physical illness or depression.

The first step in overcoming frustration and anger is to recognize that you are feeling these emotions. Many people were taught as children not to express frustration and anger. If you are feeling bottled up inside, and are not sure what to do about it, try:

- Talking with someone you trust about what you are feeling.

- Talking out loud to yourself. You can even record your voice and play it back. You can hear yourself express your feelings as though you were listening to someone else.

- Write about your feelings. Make a list of everything that is bothering you, and then decide which items you can change, and write down ways that you can change them.

- Practicing concentrated breathing and stepping back from a situation in order to get a better grip on your emotions.

- Recognizing things that you cannot change. There may be things that you can do nothing about. Simply writing them down is often helpful. Reminding yourself that some things are beyond your control also helps. This may be hard to do; you may need to remind yourself daily, or many times throughout the day, that these things are beyond your control.

- Making changes to help reduce your anger and frustration. Change the way you think from a negative to a positive perspective, to help reframe the negative feelings you are having.

If you continue to have trouble overcoming your frustration and anger, or if you have had problems with anger in the past, talk about your concerns with someone you trust, such as a member of the clergy, rabbi, chaplain, counselor, or a mental health professional. You may decide to join a self-help group or seek counseling.

Exercise:

- How would you cope when experiencing the following emotions during the grieving process? Frustration and Anger.

# ❧ CHAPTER TWELVE ❧
## Coping Techniques

"It all depends on how we look at things, and
not how they are in themselves."
~ Carl Gustav Jung

## Coping Techniques

We have seen that grief has many causes and can take many forms. Everyone reacts in their own way to loss, and it's important to pinpoint which coping techniques will work best for you. The coping techniques that we master can be very useful when dealing with situations of grief or grieving. Here are some coping techniques that can help you with the grief process:

1. When we hold on to people, things, or situations, we hurt ourselves and cannot truly be free of our grief. For many people, the philosophy of giving it to a higher source can be very comforting. It allows you to be more accepting of your loss; secure in the knowledge that everything is as it is meant to be. It is important to understand that we are not in control of the situation. Reciting a

prayer is one way to support this process. Writing and talking about it can help start the healing process, and eventually the feelings of loss become easier to handle and you can begin to move on.

2.     Sometimes we hold on to people, things, or situations out of a sense of unfinished business. We may feel upset or guilty because we did not have a chance to make amends, or to have amends made to us. We may hold on to resentments or unresolved issues that get in the way of our healing process. These issues must be resolved in order to go on with the healing process. When we realize that we can forgive ourselves or others, we heal ourselves of past hurts, resentments and grudges, and open the path for genuine healing to begin.

3.     In the end, it is up to you to take the initiative and begin to take action for your grief recovery. No one but you can know what exactly you need. Ask for help if you need it. Take good care of your body - get plenty of rest and eat right! Speak with a counselor or chaplain, if you feel that it will help you. Figure out what activities are comforting to you. Be kind to yourself if you

are depressed.   Be patient with yourself. When you are proactive about pursuing the help and healing that you need, it may help you to feel empowered and aid in the recovery process.

4.     At times of loss, it can be very helpful to be cognitive of your thinking process and how you react to your thoughts. We may experience painful trains of thought about what we've lost or find ourselves caught up in thoughts of attachment and/or regrets. Sometimes we can't break out of this cycle of negative thinking, and can even work ourselves into a deep depression or agitation. This is particularly important if you find yourself caught up in thoughts of suicide. Being aware of your thought processes allows you to take control of the thoughts that may not serve you well and replace them with more constructive ones. Gently nudging your mind away from dark thoughts and towards loving, positive thoughts is treating yourself with kindness. Rather than dwelling on your loss, it is possible to change your thoughts to remembering what was happy or joyful from the past. It will allow you to go through the

grieving process and focus on the positive things in life.

5.    When we become upset or stressed, our breathing tends to become shallow and speed up. This may prepare you to run away in the event of danger, but it is definitely counterproductive to the process of healing and recovery, which requires calm. When we are in a lot of pain, we sometimes forget to breathe. This is why practicing concentrated breathing is a key component of the grieving process. Practicing gentle and concentrated breathing is soothing and calms you down, especially after a burst of tears or strong emotions. Being aware of your breathing patterns may help reduce anxiety and fear, particularly during anticipatory grief.

6.    Accept the process of change. Remind yourself that changes, such as loss, take time to accept. It is okay to have a relapse into depression, anxiety, or anger, and to understand that these feelings are perfectly normal. It is very important to treat yourself with kindness and not to judge yourself too harshly if you are struggling with your feelings. Sometimes change is a process of

"ten steps forward and two steps back".  Rest assured that even if the grieving process happens slowly, change is still change, and you are on your way to acceptance.

7.      If we think ahead and imagine a time when our grief and grieving ends and our hearts and minds are healed, we will see that by utilizing the coping techniques described in this book, we will become aware enough to possibly avoid consequences such as losing our children, hurting our loved ones, or falling into our addictions.  In the case of the death of a loved one, you may want to imagine that your loved one is watching you right now. Is this how he or she would want you to react?

8.      Another way is to put yourself in someone else's shoes.  Ask yourself, how would Gandhi, (an advocate of peaceful resistance and contemplation) react in this situation?  How would Martin Luther King Jr. react?  Sometimes a different perspective can help us view our situation more clearly, and help us to react in healthier ways.

9.   Remembering happy times, talking about positive things, both past and future, and performing good, helpful actions are all good ways to combat loss. This may be a good time to do some volunteer work, and focus on someone less fortunate. It can give you a break from the pain of grief, and help you feel good about yourself at the same time.

10.   Attending a grief support group is another way that your positive healing words and focus, on others less fortunate, can be of help to yourself and others. It may take some time, but eventually the pain will begin to be more manageable and to ease up.

There is no perfect formula for dealing with grief and grieving. Everyone is different. Remember, life is about change, and change is often painful. Hopefully, one or more of these coping techniques will be useful in helping you to get through your time of loss. Don't ever be afraid or embarrassed to ask for help or support.

Exercise:

- Describe a time or situation in your life when you suffered a painful loss. How did you cope with your feelings of grief and grieving?

- Which coping techniques do you think you could have used in that situation? Do you think that your results would have been different or the same?

- Which coping techniques would you use to handle the following emotions during the grieving process and why?

1. Sadness and Yearning:

2. Worry and Anxiety:

3. Feelings of Guilt:

4. Frustration and Anger:

# ❧ CHAPTER THIRTEEN ❧
## The Healing Process

*"Our sorrows and wounds are healed only when we touch them with compassion."*
~ Buddha

## The Healing Process

There are three important areas of our being that can be affected in an adverse way during our period of grief and mourning. Through a better understanding of the grieving process and by using coping techniques we have learned, we can protect, nurture, and heal these areas. They are our; Emotional well being, Physical well being, and Spiritual well being. All three areas are interconnected in a way that you may not have been aware of and one can have a profound effect on the others.

For most of us, we tend to separate these three areas of our being into separate boxes. We have one box for our emotions, one for our physical bodies, and one for our spiritual thoughts and beliefs. We believe that our physical bodies; organs and systems are totally separate from our thoughts, emotions, and our spiritual, faith and belief, based selves. In this chapter we will explore how our emotions and thoughts can affect our physical bodies, and how our values and beliefs can affect our everyday health and our spiritual well being. Our emotions, physical being, and spirit, together form the whole person. Our body is the vessel that houses all of our organs, systems, brain, mind, emotions, and spirit. Spirit, in the sense of our being in the state of good or calm spirit, emotionally balanced, and physically sound. Some may refer to our spirit as our soul, based on beliefs and traditions. For our purposes of defining the healing process for our whole being we will refer to these as emotional, physical, and spiritual.

This chapter is not about anatomy, physiology, disease, religious, or spiritual beliefs. It is about recognizing how all three of these areas can affect the others in preventing us from, or permitting us to, move through the grieving process and helping us achieve a purposeful, peaceful life beyond our grief.

## Emotional Healing

For us to heal our emotional wounds, we must first acknowledge that we are hurting. There is no doubt that through our grief and grieving there are painful emotional wounds that need healing. Just our sadness and yearning for a loved one, or lifestyle that we have lost, causes us to hurt. We can transfer this pain to our bodies as well. Emotional healing can play a key role in our physical healing process. When we worry or hold on to fears and anxiety we create dis-comfort and dis-ease in our bodies, manifested through shortness of breath, nervousness, emotional restlessness, lack of sleep, pacing, twitches in our bodies, due to nervousness, or unconscious motor sensory actions, i.e., biting our nails, tugging on our hair, repetitive actions, etc. Eventually these emotions and actions can wear our bodies down and cause our autoimmune system to kick in to counteract the stress, dis-comfort, and dis-ease that the body is experiencing. Can you see how our emotions can affect our bodies?

Our feelings come to us automatically. It is very difficult to choose which feelings we experience, because our emotions react and give us instant feedback about how a particular situation or person is affecting us. They are, in a sense, our warning mechanism. However, we have the ability to recognize them as not only a warning mechanism, but as a censor mechanism as well. Fear can create instant anxiety and our physical bodies can chemically produce an adrenalin rush (Epinephrine) to assist us in moving out of the way of a speeding car, bus, or train, and out of harm's way. It is up to us then to move emotionally out of that state of fear, once the danger has passed. We can do this by being aware that the danger has passed and calming ourselves down emotionally, thus allowing our body to stop producing adrenalin and returning to a normal physical state. We can achieve this by doing calming breathing techniques and relaxing coping techniques, that we discussed in earlier chapters. If we remain in a state of fear, worry, or anxiety, our bodies will continue to chemically respond with un-needed adrenalin and other chemicals. We are not made physically to sustain this physical or emotional state of being over a prolonged period of time.

There are two basic underlying emotions in all human beings with varying degrees of intensity. They are love and fear. Desire, joy, pleasure, contentment, acceptance, hope, peacefulness, excitement, self-esteem, and generosity are a few examples of love-based feelings. Anxiety, anger, sorrow, apathy, bitterness, jealousy, irritability, depression, rejection, self-pity, grief, aggressiveness, powerlessness, loneliness, and irritability are examples of fear-based emotions. Different chemicals are produced by our bodies when we feel these two groups of emotions. We have discussed how our body reacts to the latter emotions of fear and anxiety, which as you can see can cause extreme stress on our systems.

Our brains control what chemicals our bodies release in response to our emotions. Some of the chemicals that our brains release such as Serotonin and Dopamine, as well as, the amino acid Tryptophan, also play a significant role in our physical and mental state. Endorphin, a body's natural pain reliever and Serotonin, a hormone responsible for happiness, help the brain cure pain and sadness respectively.  In contrast, Serotonin and Nor-epinephrine are the main chemicals in the brain which cause depression. Studies have shown that low Serotonin levels in the brain can lead to anxiety, irritability and sleep disorders, which are normally associated with depression. Similarly, studies have shown that reduced levels of Nor-epinephrine, a chemical responsible for arousal and alertness, can lead to fatigue and a general depressed mood.

Dopamine is another chemical in the brain which can cause depression in a few cases. This particular neurotransmitter is associated with rewards that a person would get if he or she continues participating in a particular activity. Another fact about Dopamine is that it is associated with addiction. Alcohol or drugs can stimulate its production in the body. An imbalance of any of these chemicals can have an affect not only on our emotions, but on our bodies as well, leading to an imbalance in our whole being. Chemical imbalances lead to undue stress, worry and nervousness. But it is because of such emotions people know how to laugh, cry, love or worry. Chemical imbalances are an integral part of human nature, which help in interpreting and reacting to different situations, and hence cannot be avoided. This brief, simple description of how the brain produces certain chemicals is for informational purposes only and to give you, the reader, a better understanding of the correlation between the mind and the body as they can at times work in tandem to produce positive or negative affects in the whole being. I highly recommend that you seek guidance from a professional medical doctor or psychologist for interpreting any chemical or physiological levels in your body. This book is not designed to be used for self-treatment. The information is not intended or implied to be a substitute for professional medical advice or a replacement for any treatment.

Emotional healing begins when we become aware of our thoughts and how they affect our whole being. When we become aware of our thoughts, we can make a determination at that time how to respond. If we have a negative thought, we can pause, take a breath, and then replace that thought with a positive one. Create a positive thought (wedge) between the negative thought and that part of our brain that reacts in a negative way. We can then redirect the neurons to a positive part of our brain that reacts in a positive way. The key to emotional healing is allowing yourself to feel the emotions, control them, let them pass, and move on. Allow yourself the time to grieve. Use the tools and coping techniques you have learned in previous chapters, and remember that the emotions that you are experiencing are a normal part of the grieving process. Practice meditating on positive thoughts, and releasing negative thoughts and false realities. Monitor your breathing and your mental and physical responses. Calming your mind will calm your body. Controlling your emotions will control your body as well.

## Physical Healing

We now know a little bit more about the cause and effect, grief and grieving has in creating emotional wounds, and also the emotional pain and hurt we experience as a result. Sometimes we can feel this hurt or pain not only in our emotional hearts and minds, but in our physical body as well. We feel hurt in our body, in the form of; aches and pains, shortness of breath, nausea, chills, twitches or shaking, etc. We know that tension can cause headaches, fear can cause shortness of breath, nervousness can cause sweaty palms and upset stomachs, etc. It is clear that there is a definite relationship between our emotional and our physical self. So how do we heal ourselves physically? First, as we discussed in the previous section, we start the emotional healing process. Combining both physical and emotional (mental) exercises together at the same time, such as, Yoga, Tai-Chi, Reiki, walking, jogging, hiking, swimming, bike riding, dancing, exercises, i.e., isometrics, weightlifting, etc., can help us to stimulate the mind and the body in a very positive way. (Check with a physician or physical education coach before embarking on any physical exercise programs that you are not used to doing , or you are not familiar with.)

While creating a positive environment for creative thoughts, and at the same time, providing the physical stimulation to work our muscles, get our blood flowing to the cells and areas of our bodies that need healing the most, and helping us control our breathing and respiration, allowing oxygen to flow into our lungs, any of these activities will help heal both your mind and your body. The connection between emotions (mind) and body will become very apparent as you practice these tools. If you are not used to doing much exercise, you should start slowly. Do not push yourself into something that will cause you more physical pain. Join a beginner's meet-up group or beginner's yoga studio, or just take a nice easy stroll along a beach, or a pathway at your local park. The important thing is to get out and get some fresh air and exercise, to clear your mind.

Massage is a good form of relaxation and muscle rejuvenation. Taking a nice, relaxing, and soothing mineral bath and listening to relaxing, meditative music can be very helpful in the healing process. As you become more skilled at your chosen means of mental and physical release and exercise, you will start to see a change not only in the way you view yourself emotionally, but also physically. Sometimes, but most often, we find ourselves too wrapped up in our grieving to realize that the rest of the world is moving around us and we are standing still. A wise doctor once shared something with me that he said to one of his patients one day. He said, "You have two choices". "You can stay in bed all day depressed… or you can get up, get dressed, go out, and do something. Either way you will still be depressed, but at least if you get up and go out, and do something, there is a possibility you can accomplish great things!" He told me, after hearing that, his patient was up bright and early every morning anticipating the new day and the many positive things it had in store for him. Sometimes, it is as simple as that. The body and the mind, the physical and the emotional, are very much connected.

Nutrition plays a key role in helping us remain physically and emotionally balanced. There is a very close relationship between nutrition from foods and neurological (electrical) impulses that help the brain function. Also our body's muscles and tissues require good nutrients to sustain and regenerate themselves. Our bodies require fuel in the form of food and nutrients to function. Since our body is the vessel (container) that houses our organs, systems, brain, mind, emotions, and spirit, it would make sense to insure that we are providing this vessel with the most care and nutrients that it needs to function. Good nutrition and a balanced diet are essential for both emotional and physical healing.

## Spiritual Healing

A person's spiritual nature is one of a non-physical nature. This could include his or her, mind, thoughts, emotions, life force, soul, or spirit. Spiritual healing does not require a person to follow a certain belief or religion. A person's spirituality could be based on one's values, beliefs, or traditions, but that is not a requirement. One must only accept the belief that their whole being is something other than just physical, that there are facets of one's being that go beyond the physical aspect.

Spiritual Healing can refer to a realization, a quest, or a journey, along an inner path, enabling a person to discover the essence of his or her being; or it can also represent the deepest values and meanings by which people live. Spiritual discovery or practices, including creative visualization, meditation, prayer and contemplation, are intended to develop an individual's inner life, soul, or spirit. Spiritual healing enables a person to connect with a larger reality, discovering a new self, connecting with nature or the universe, or with divinity.

When our emotions, body, mind, and soul are in synchronization, our whole being is in balance and our spirit is healed. Practices such as; Yoga, Reiki, meditation, prayer, and contemplation, create a peaceful and serene mental and physical state in which to explore our inner pathway and connection with our inner true identity and purpose. Through spiritual healing we can find direction in our lives. As we contemplate memories and past events in a calm and peaceful way, we give rise to new wisdom and understanding. As we become cognizant (aware) of our emotions, responses, and behaviors, we give rise to better, more positive solutions in our daily lives. Feeling a connection to the universe or to a divine existence removes the loneliness, or hopelessness, that we have experienced in the past due to a loss in our lives.

Spiritual healing is a pathway to a higher state of awareness, perfection of one's own whole being, and a connection with the divine self. It is the development of inner peace, happiness, and personal well being. As we explore our emotions through the grief and grieving process, we become more aware and in tune with what it is that makes us tick. How we respond to situations and others. How we respond to loss and change. When we embrace the process of grieving and allow ourselves to heal emotionally, physically, and spiritually, we naturally grow internally as a result of our experiences. New thoughts, ideas, and opportunities open up for us. New relationships develop, and older relationships become more solid and meaningful. A strong foundation is developed, which is essential for the management and understanding of thoughts and emotions, which otherwise prevent happiness.

I encourage you to seek guidance and knowledge through your own research and discovery, as well as, available resources to help you navigate the pathway to inner peace, happiness, and spiritual healing. There are many sources of inspiration available and you must choose which inspires and heals you the most.

Exercise:

- Describe some emotions that you have experienced in the past that have prevented you from moving forward with your emotional healing process.

- How have your emotions affected your physical body? Have you experienced any physical problems that can be attributed to your emotional state?

- What are your spiritual beliefs and how would the way you feel about yourself and your spirituality help you heal your emotions, body, and spirit?

# ✎ CHAPTER FOURTEEN ✎
## Living Beyond Loss

*"Although the world is full of suffering, it is also full of the overcoming of it."*
*~ Helen Keller*

## Adjusting to a New Life

Adjusting to loss starts when you accept the loss and become determined to live beyond it. Believing you can create a new life for yourself may not be easy, but it is certainly attainable. The fact is that "Life must go on." It is up to us as individuals to decide how we choose to live our lives and how we choose to move on after a loss. Accept that life is for the living. It takes effort to begin to live again in the present and not dwell on the past. Sometimes it is best to postpone major life changes until you feel the time is right and you are ready. Try to hold off on making any major changes, such as moving, remarrying, changing jobs or having another child until you feel confident that you are not making choices based on the emotions generated by your loss. If you are sure that the decisions you are making are of sound judgment, of sound mind, body, and spirit, then by all means move forward with confidence. If you are not sure or hesitant, or if you are not of sound mind, body, or spirit, then you should give yourself more time to adjust to your loss. Seek out the advice of a qualified counselor or therapist before making any decisions that will affect the rest of your life.

The grief and grieving process can go on as long as you need it to, but in the end, you will find it necessary to pick yourself back up, and create a new life. The good news is, your new life is there waiting for you to create it. If you are not living alone, then it's a matter of beginning anew with your family members, partner, roommate, children, or those living under your roof. It is time to make the decision to embrace them and your new acceptance, and your desire to let go of the grief and move forward. Helping them with their grieving process can help you start the process of creating a new life, or securing a strong foundation in your and their lives again. Begin by making the changes necessary to move everyone forward. Perhaps start group, couple, or family activities again. Bring things into the normal range of acceptance and behavior. Sometimes, after the loss of a loved one, just getting through a day is a real accomplishment, but gradually, ever so gradually, the will to move on, the will to live, usually kicks in. Sometimes lifestyle changes may even be necessary. But, if somehow the ones left behind can look at life as a potential for new possibilities, then maybe, just maybe, something good can result from a painful loss.

Even though we cannot change the past and bring back the one we loved, we have a choice to live life in spite of death, in spite of new circumstances. We have a choice to look for a new dream, maybe even a new path, and to approach life as a "potential for new possibilities."

## Living Alone

If you have lost your spouse or life partner and you find yourself living alone or if your friends and family seem to have moved on with their lives and are giving you less support, you may be feeling very lonely and lost. Just preparing a meal for one person after preparing or sharing a meal with someone can be a sad and overwhelming experience.

Going to bed alone at night or waking up in the morning with no one by your side, after sharing your bed and sleep time with someone close to you, can also create anxiety and leave you with feelings of abandonment. Whether you have had time to prepare for the loss of a spouse, or not, living alone for the first time in a long time can be lonely, confusing and frustrating.

It can be pretty quiet in a house with one person. No distractions or sounds other than the sound of your own thoughts interrupting your sleep or concentration. You can now do anything that you have ever wanted to do, without being discouraged by your well meaning spouse or significant other. However, because of your grief and loss, none of that seems to matter anymore. It is time now to understand that your personal well being is of the utmost importance, and that taking care of your health and peace of mind is your top priority.

If the quietness is making you feel more lonely or anxious, you can have some friends over or invite them out for a day or a night on the town. If you can't think of a reason to have people over, create one. Invite some friends over and prepare a dinner, or have a home movie night. Go out to a restaurant or a show.

Try a new hobby by joining a group that sounds interesting to you. Perhaps you want to take a class. Keep in mind that nothing you start needs to be finished. You can decide to shift interests anytime you want to. Sample a taste of something new and then decide if you want to continue. Just start.

Keep your mind open, and be willing to consider some new concepts. Be aware of the fact that you are living in a time when there is an abundance of options that you may not have ever heard of before. Think outside of the box. Try something that you have no experience with. Find a group that meditates or does yoga. Instead of walking for exercise, find a group that hikes.

It is up to you to fill your life with abundance. You are starting over, in many ways, but this time you are more mature, wiser, and experienced. Things may be different than what you have been used to, but you can make your life as meaningful as you did in the past and more so. Happiness can have a new meaning, and the route will be more direct and simpler to find. When you are ready to make the shift, know that the world is waiting for you.

## Loving Again

There are no guarantees in this life. When a loved one enters our life, there is no surety for how long he or she will stay. They're not possessions to be owned, but rather our gift to be cherished for as long as we have them. When someone we love leaves us, it creates a huge void in our lives. If love is what we lost, then the only thing that will help us to feel better is more love. During this time you may confuse sex with love and go looking for meaningless encounters. However, this again will only postpone the inevitability of the pain of the loss of love. Eventually, you will realize that this is no substitute for the pain of loss you are experiencing. You may feel that you cannot or should not love again, because that would be an injustice to the loved one that died. This could not be further from the truth.

We all have in us an intrinsic, almost instinctive, need to love and be loved. We must replace love with love. Reach out to friends, family and co-workers, anyone who will fill some of the gap left by your loved one. It's not the same, it's not what you are really craving, but it will help heal the pain. It is okay to love again. After reaching out to those who love us, you can then start rebuilding your life and your strength. You can go on. You can laugh again. And yes, you can love again.

Love has many forms. You may develop another relationship in time. You may find a cause that you love and believe in. You may find or create work you love. You may get a pet that you can love unconditionally. You may become involved in the lives of your extended family. Whatever form love takes, it will fill the void that was left from the relationship you lost. Allow yourself to love yourself. Believe that you are worthy of love and to be loved.

## Reinventing Yourself after Loss

If you are at a turning point in your life, whether you have just been through a divorce or separation, or have experienced a loss in your life, lost your job, or a loved one, it is the perfect time to start reinventing yourself. Reinvention is: A chance for renewal and the opportunity to change. Reinventing is a significant, noteworthy movement from point A to point B, for whatever point A and point B represent for you.

Reinventing represents a departure from what came before, or an embellishment of something that was in place. Often even the most positive change represents upheaval. Upheaval: not in the negative sense, but in the positive action of stirring up the dust and changing old habits and seeing what's left when the dust clears.

Reinvention can be a willingness to be more open to roles outside of your normal comfort zone or niche. On the flip side, it can be a willingness to narrow your scope and focus on your very specific dream. In other words, figure out what's missing for you and then address it. Since there is no time like the present to start a new life after a loss, you have the opportunity to be the person you always wanted to be. Transform your present situation, or perhaps make a career change. Complete those classes you meant to finish years ago, or start a new hobby or interest, find a new romance or travel and see the world. I recommend that you read more on the subject of "Reinventing" either on-line, or you can pick up a book at your local book store, or library, on the subject. Change takes time, patience, work, persistence, and faith in your-self. Above all: believe in yourself and do not let anyone tell you, "You can't change."

Your dreams can come true. We each have the power within us to make change occur. You need only to look within and tap that part of your inner self that wants you to be happy again. And all things are possible.

Exercise:

- Describe how it will feel emotionally to you, adjusting to a new life beyond loss.

- How would you feel about living alone?

- How would you feel about loving again?

- What does reinvention mean to you?

# A Few More Thoughts

There is an old Chinese proverb by Lao Tzu, author of the "Tao Te Ching", and who, according to Chinese tradition, lived in the 6th century BCE; that says, "Some roads aren't meant to be traveled alone."

Although loss can affect us in a very personal way, and navigating through the grief and grieving process can become a personal journey of recovery and acceptance, we do not have to travel that road alone. We can choose to reach out to those around us, to seek support and comfort from someone you trust, such as a friend or family member, member of the clergy, rabbi, chaplain, counselor, or a mental health professional. You may decide to join a self-help or grief support group, or seek counseling. There is no shame, dishonor or embarrassment, in seeking the help and support you need to travel this road as you journey. Remember, it is perfectly acceptable and important to get the support that you need.

Many individuals face the torment, anguish, and pain of loss alone, not having the knowledge or understanding of what they are experiencing, and not aware of the many support resources that are available to them. Hopefully, after reading this book on grief and the grieving process, you will have a better understanding of what you or your loved ones are personally going though and you will be motivated and encouraged to get more information from other sources, and seek the support that you may need.

The healing of a broken heart and the grieving process may take some time, and the journey may be a long one, but the road we choose and the way we travel that road, our attitude and understanding, can make all the difference in the world. We do not have to travel that road alone, or without the proper provisions to sustain us. If we stumble, we can pick our self up and dust our self off and continue on our journey. If we grow weary, we can rest, rejuvenate, and nourish our body, mind, and spirit, and find the strength to continue on our journey. Failure or turning back does not have to be a solution to our struggle. Know that a brief delay is just that, a brief delay, and once we realize this, we can move forward again with confidence.

I recall another old Chinese saying, author unknown, but some attribute it to Confucius; that says, "The journey of a thousand miles begins with one step."

Honor yourself, and your journey, and honor others for their journeys. Allow yourself to move forward in this process, taking one step at a time, until you have reached your destination of acceptance, peace of mind, and happiness. May you find happiness, joy, peace of mind, and contentment in your life once again, wherever your journey may lead you.

# Glossary

**Addiction** - Drug dependence. A state of physiological or psychological dependence on a potentially harmful drug.

**Adrenalin** – Adrenalin Rush; An adrenaline rush is the fight-or-flight response of the adrenal gland, in which it releases adrenaline (epinephrine).

**Affirmation** - An assertion of support or agreement. A positive statement and/or a declaration of the truth or existence of something.

**Ambivalence** - The presence of two opposing ideas, attitudes, or emotions at the same time. A feeling of uncertainty about something due to a mental conflict

**Anger** - A strong feeling of grievance and displeasure. To become or make somebody extremely annoyed.

**Anguish** - Extreme anxiety or emotional torment.

**Anticipatory** – In expectation of something, experienced or done in the expectation of a future event.

**Anticipatory Grief** - Grief that strikes in advance of an impending loss.

**Anxiety** – Feeling of worry, nervousness or agitation, often about something that is going to happen. A subject or concern, that causes worry.

**Autoimmune** – Autoimmunity is the condition in which the body's immune system produces antibodies in response to its own tissues or blood components instead of foreign particles or microorganisms.

**Autonomic** - (Autonomic Nervous System) The portion of the nervous system concerned with regulation of activity of cardiac muscle, smooth muscle, and glands, usually restricted to the sympathetic and parasympathetic nervous systems.

**Bargaining** - An agreement between two people or groups in which each promises to carry out an obligation. To make a pact with someone, including one's self.

**Bereavement** – To bereave is to deprive somebody of a beloved person or a treasured thing, especially through death. The act of bereaving.

**Bipolar Disorder** - A psychiatric disorder characterized by extreme mood swings, ranging between episodes of acute euphoria, mania, and severe depression.

**Cardiovascular System** - Of or relating to the heart and the blood vessels.

**Caregiver** - Somebody who has the principal responsibility for caring for a child or dependent adult, especially in the home.

**Chaplain** - A member of the clergy employed to give religious guidance, e.g. to members of the armed forces, school children, or prisoners.

**Clergy** - The body of people ordained for religious service, especially in the Christian church.

**Complicated Grief** - An abnormal response to bereavement that includes unrelieved yearning for the deceased person, the complete loss of previous positive beliefs or world views, and a general inability to function.

**Counselor** - Somebody, usually a professional, who helps others with personal, social, or psychological problems. A professional who gives advice on such matters as careers, education, or health.

**Confucius** - (551-479 BCE), Confucius according to Chinese tradition, was a thinker, political figure, educator, and founder of the Ru School of Chinese thought.

**Depression** - A state of unhappiness and hopelessness. A psychiatric disorder showing symptoms such as persistent feelings of hopelessness, dejection, poor concentration, lack of energy, inability to sleep, and, sometimes, suicidal tendencies.

**Diary** - A personal book or record of events in somebody's life, often including personal thoughts and observations.

**Divorce** - An ending of a marriage by an official decision in a court of law. A complete separation or split.

**Dopamine** – A chemical compound occurring in the brain. A neurotransmitter that is also a precursor of epinephrine.

**Elisabeth Kübler-Ross** – MD (July 8, 1926 – August 24, 2004) was a psychiatrist, a pioneer in Near-death studies and the author of the groundbreaking book On Death and Dying (1969), where she first discussed what is now known as the Kübler-Ross model.

**Endocrine** - Relating to the endocrine glands or their secretions. A hormone.

**Endorphin** - A substance in the brain that attaches to the same cell receptors that morphine does. Endorphins are released when severe injury occurs, often abolishing all sensation of pain.

**Epinephrine** - A synthetic form of adrenaline. Use: to relax the airways and constrict blood vessels.

**Fear** - An unpleasant feeling of anxiety or apprehension caused by the presence or anticipation of danger.

**Frustration** - A feeling of disappointment, exasperation, or weariness caused by goals being thwarted or desires unsatisfied.

**Gandhi** - Revered in India as the "Father of the Nation," Mohandas K. Gandhi is also a worldwide icon of non-violent political resistance. He was born October 1869 and died at the hands of an assassin in January 1948. Also known as Mahatma Gandhi.

**Getting Out By Going in Organization** - A non-profit organization dedicated to helping at-risk men, women, and children make better life choices, and lasting positive changes and successes. (GOGI).

**Grief** - Great sadness, especially as a result of a death. The cause of intense, deep, and profound sorrow, especially a specific event or situation.

**Guilt** - Awareness real or perceived of having done wrong or committed a crime, accompanied by feelings of shame and regret.

**Hallucinatory** - Relating to or involving the belief that something is being seen, heard, or otherwise sensed when it is not present or actually occurring at the time.

**Heinous** – A shockingly evil or wicked act or crime.

**Immune System** - The interacting combination of all the body's ways of recognizing cells, tissues, objects, and organisms that are not part of itself, and initiating the immune response to fight them.

**Incapacitated** – Present state of depriving or being deprived of power, force, or effectiveness. A state of illness or restriction that does not allow a person to move about in a normal fashion.

**Insomnia** - Inability to fall asleep or to remain asleep long enough to feel rested, especially when this is a problem that continues over time.

**Internet** - A network that links computer networks all over the world by satellite and telephone, connecting users with service networks such as e-mail and the World Wide Web.

**Judicial** - Relating or belonging to a body of judges or to the system that administers justice.

**Martin Luther King Jr.** – Born January 15, 1929 and died at the hands of an assassin on April 4, 1968) Martin Luther King Jr. was an American clergyman, activist, and prominent leader in the African-American Civil Rights Movement. He is best known for being an iconic figure in the advancement of civil rights in the United States and around the world, using nonviolent methods following the teachings of Mahatma Gandhi.

**Meditation** – The act of emptying the mind of thoughts, or the concentration of the mind on one thing, in order to aid mental or spiritual development, contemplation, or relaxation.

**Mourning** – To mourn a loss. The feeling or showing of deep sadness following somebody's death. The period during which somebody's death is mourned.

**Physiological** - Relating to the way that living things function, rather than to their shape or structure.

**Post Traumatic Stress Disorder** – PTSD. A psychological condition affecting people who have suffered severe emotional trauma as a result of an experience such as combat, crime, or natural disaster, and causing sleep disturbances, flashbacks, anxiety, tiredness, and depression.

**Prefrontal Cortex** – At the very front of the brain, relating to or situated in the foremost part of the brain, in front of the frontal bone.

**Psychologist** - A professional who studies behavior and experience, and who is licensed to provide therapeutic services or to work in an academic setting.

**Reiki** - In alternative medicine, a treatment in which healing energy is channeled from the practitioner to the patient to enhance energy and reduce stress, pain, and fatigue.

**Reinventing** - To invent something again, or bring something back into existence, use, or popularity after a period of neglect or obscurity. To radically change the appearance, form, or presentation of something or somebody.

**Self-Awareness** - Having a balanced and honest view of your own personality, and often an ability to interact with others frankly and confidently.

**Serotonin** - A chemical derived from the amino acid tryptophan and widely distributed in tissues. It acts as a neurotransmitter, constricts blood vessels at injury sites, and may affect emotional states.

**Sorrow** - A feeling of deep sadness caused by a loss or misfortune. To feel or express deep sadness over something.

**Spirituality** - The quality or condition of being spiritual. Relating to the soul or spirit, usually in contrast to material things

**Sudden Infant Death Syndrome** – (SIDS) A fatal condition that affects sleeping infants that are less than one year old and appear to be healthy. It is characterized by a sudden cessation of breathing and is thought to be caused by a defect in the central nervous system. Also called crib death, or SIDS.

**Tai Chi** - A Chinese form of physical exercise characterized by a series of very slow and deliberate balletic body movements.

**Trauma** - An extremely distressing experience that causes severe emotional shock and may have long-lasting psychological effects. A physical injury or wound to the body.

**Tryptophan** - An essential amino acid found in proteins such as casein and fibrin.

**Worry** - To feel anxious about something unpleasant that may have happened or may happen. To feel annoyed or to annoy somebody.

**Yearning** – A strong desire, often tinged with sadness.

**Yoga** - a Hindu discipline that promotes spiritual unity with a supreme being through a system of postures and rituals. A system or set of breathing exercises and postures derived from or based on Hindu yoga

# Index

# Index (continued)

# Index (continued)

## Index (continued)

# Index (continued)

# Index (continued)

# References

Internet sites and research material referenced in:  Grief and Grieving
Understanding Grief and the Grieving Process

American Board of Hypnotherapy (ABH)
http://abh-abnlp.com/

American Society for Psychical Research (ASPR) http://www.aspr.com/

Anger definition researched online at:
http://en.wikipedia.org/wiki/Anger

Anger and Frustration definition researched online at:
http://en.wikipedia.org/wiki/Frustration

Anticipatory Grief and managing sadness and depression definitions researched online at:
http://www.webmd.com 2010 Web

Dr.  Melvin M.  Moore, Ph.D. Clinical and Consulting Psychologist Executive Director, Secure Transitions Inc.

Glossary references in part researched at:
http://medical=dictionary.thefreedictionary.
com and The Encarta Dictionary: English
(North America 2007)

Additional glossary references:
Confucius glossary reference: Riegel, Jeffrey,
"Confucius", *The Stanford Encyclopedia of
Philosophy (Spring 2011 Edition)*, Edward N.
Zalta (ed.), http://plato.stanford.edu/
archives/spr2011/entries/confucius/

Gandhi glossary reference:
http://www.answers.com/topic/mohandas-
gandhi

Martin Luther King Jr. glossary reference:
http://en.wikipedia.org/wiki/Martin_Luther
_King,_Jr

Grief and Grieving researched online at:
health.yahoo.com/mentalhealth-
overview/grief-and-grieving/healthwise.
2009. Web

Grief Process – Practical Instructions:
allaboutlifechallenges.org/grief-process 2009
Web

Guilt definition researched online at: http://en.wikipedia.org/wiki/Guilt 2010 Web

"Guilt." Encyclopedia of Psychology. 2nd ed. Ed. Bonnie R. Strickland. Gale Group, Inc., 2001. eNotes.com. 2006. 31 December 2007

Hypnosis Society of Alberta (HSA) http://hypnosissociety.org/Index.html

International Hypnosis Federation (IHF) http://www.internationalhypnosisfederation. com/

Living Alone and Loving Again researched online at: http://ezinearticles.com 2011 Web

Managing Grief: researched online at: revolutionhealth.com/healthy-living 2009

Quotes and historical sayings researched on-line at: http://www.quoteland.com/topic.asp and at: http://www.brainyquote.com/ and http://www.finestquotes.com/select_quote-category

Reverend Doctor Mara Leigh "Coach" Taylor Ph.D.  Founder and Executive Director, Getting out by Going in Organization

Sadness and Yearning definitions – Encarta Dictionary (North American) source 2007.

Sadness and Yearning definitions researched at: Stages of Mourning after Death/ehow.com http://www.ehow.com/list_6152518_stages-mourning-after-death.html

Signs of Sadness researched at: http://www.ehow.com/about 2011 Web

Stages of Grieving: Elisabeth Kubler-Ross in her 1969 book, *On Death and Dying*.

Sudden Infant Death Sydrome: Source: National SIDS Resource Center - September 1997

Videbeck, Sheila L. (2006.). *Psychiatric Mental Health Nursing* (3rd Ed.). Lippincott Williams & Wilkins

Wikipedia research: http://en.wikipedia.org

# About the Author

Daniel Wheeler is a management professional and corporate coach. He is a registered and certified hypnotherapist, lecturer, writer, published composer, international recording artist, life coach, and workshop instructor. He is also an ordained minister, and certified spiritual counselor. He is a past member of the American Board of Hypnotherapy, the Alberta Hypnosis Society, and The International Hypnosis Federation. He is recognized as a stage and media personality. Daniel Wheeler is also a Fellow with The American Society for Psychical Research. He is certified in advanced clinical hypnotherapy techniques, Time Line Therapy™, and Regression Therapy. Daniel Wheeler is a certified Reiki Practitioner. He is also certified as a Spiritual Hypnotherapy Specialist.

Daniel Wheeler has over sixteen years experience as a Hypnotherapist and Life Coach. He specializes in weight loss and smoking cessation programs, and has a success rate of greater than 90%. He is further acknowledged as an expert in the area of re-inventing oneself through self-hypnosis, which he teaches through group and individual programs and workshops.

Daniel Wheeler provides individual and group life coaching, corporate coaching, as well as hypnotherapy and self-help services for vocational purposes. He conducts workshops and seminars on personal growth, career motivation, and professional growth. He also conducts individual and group Reiki training and services, and intuitive training workshops. Daniel lectures at various health and wellness expos on a variety of subjects. Daniel is also a Certified Coach and Instructor for the Getting Out By Going In Organization, a 501c non-profit organization dedicated to helping at-risk men, women, and children make better life choices, supporting inmate education, reform and self-awareness, and is a past member of the GOGI Board of Advisors.

Daniel Wheeler is acclaimed as a dynamic presenter on topics ranging from personal growth, self-hypnosis, and intuitive training, to career motivation and professional growth, both for the individual client and for corporations. His unique presentation style is both entertaining and very informative. An accomplished musician and composer, Daniel Wheeler, on occasion, provides voice-overs and background music compositions. He has produced various compact disc recordings for counselors and self-help practitioners (i.e., Yoga and Reiki teachers, practitioners, and hypnotherapists).

As an international recording artist, Daniel Wheeler has recorded and published fourteen original meditation and music compact discs available in several countries. He performs live music for entertainment at various locations and venues.

As the Founder and Executive Director of Horizon Consulting and Productions, Daniel Wheeler can be reached at info@horizpro.com or visit his website at www.horizpro.com.

Or write to:
Daniel Wheeler/Horizon Consulting
P.O. Box 283, Lomita, CA 90717, USA

# Notes:

# Notes:

# Notes:

Notes:

www.ingramcontent.com/pod-product-compliance
Lightning Source LLC
LaVergne TN
LVHW011231080426
835509LV00005B/441